COUNTRY CHURCHYARDS
IN WALES

Donald Gregory

Gwasg Carreg Gwalch

ISBN: 0-86381-183-3

Maps by K. Lloyd Gruffydd

Cover design: Anne Lloyd Morris

First published in 1991 by Gwasg Carreg Gwalch,

Llangwm Churchyards in Clwyd (top), Gwent (middle) and Dyfed (bottom).
All 3 churches are dedicated to St Jerome

To the unknown Welshman, who, when approached at a bus stop by the author with the plea "Where am I? I'm lost" replied, with a smile, "Boyo, you're not lost. You've got me," and proceeded to set me on my way.

By the same author:
"Wales Before 1066 — A Guide"
"Yesterday in Village Church and Churchyard"

CONTENTS

Foreword 8

PART 1

1   Burial through the ages 10
2   Churchyards on prehistoric sites 16
3   Roman remains in churchyards 23
4   Holy wells 26
5   Early Christian memorial stones 34
6   Yew Trees 40
7   The organisation of the churchyard 44
8   Early nonconformist burial grounds 54

PART 2   A REGIONAL SURVEY

1   GWYNEDD AND CLWYD

A   Anglesey 62
B   The Pilgrims' route to Bardsey 71
C   Here and there in Gwynedd 80
D   The Northern Marches 88

2   POWYS

A   The Central Marches 95
B   West of the Teme 103
C   East of the Wye 112
D   Brecon and the Black Mountains 121

3   GWENT AND GLAMORGAN

A   The Southern Marches 129
B   St Illtud country 138
C   The Gower Peninsula 145

4   DYFED

A   Around Haverfordwest 153
B   Between Preseli and the sea 160
C   In old Cardiganshire 167

Bibliography 174
Acknowledgements 174
Index 175

FOREWORD

More than a hundred and thirty ancient monuments of considerable historical importance will be dealt with in these pages, that being the number of churchyards to be visited. Churchyards are generally older than the churches they surround and are therefore of even greater value to the social historian; they provide to the discerning enquirer much evidence of local activity in times when the church was the very centre of parish life and when the churchyard was the village playground, church and churchyard together furnishing the locality with a community centre. Even in the closing years of the twentieth century the Bronze Age pattern of settlement in some parts of Wales, fifteen hundred years and more before the birth of Christ, can still be detected by a patient enquiry into the relationship of a churchyard to its immediate neighbourhood, particularly where prehistoric wells and stone monuments were in later days made holy by Christian priests and thereafter brought into Christian use.

One of the objects of this book is to convince readers, who may think of rural churchyards in Wales as gloomy and neglected places, that on the contrary they are places where careful study may reveal much of the early social history of Wales, despite the long grass and the rusty gates and the general air of neglect and gloom. This necessary attempt at an imaginative investigation must not be long delayed; if unfortunately it should be, much of the fast fading evidence will have disappeared for ever. Shortage of clergy, changes in religious habits and rural depopulation have greatly speeded up the decaying process in many churchyards in Wales. Even in the lifetime of the author a number of well-tended churchyards have fallen into such decay that sometimes a map reference is now needed to find the locality, where not so many years ago a thriving community flourished.

It must be stressed that it is impossible as well as undesirable to separate churchyards in this book from their churches; the emphasis has clearly to be on the churchyard, but the church will not altogether be ignored, especially as its social function so often merged into that of the churchyard. For, when the weather intervened, social activities that normally went on in the unconsecrated north side of the churchyard, were frequently transferred to the nave of the church, which likewise remained unsanctified throughout the Middle Ages. Furthermore the early Christian missionaries, St David, Teilo, Illtud, Beuno and their peers, were all as much associated with the churchyards as with the churches, so many of which still bear in their dedications their honoured names.

In the second — and longer — part of this book Wales has been divided into its administrative areas and then subdivided on a regional basis. As it is impossible for the author to offer a worthwhile guide to all the churchyards in Wales there has to be some limitation. He has chosen to ignore churchyards in cities and large towns in a necessary attempt to avoid crowding his canvas. One final word. What follows is the choice of one enthusiast, who has had to make a selection. He seeks the forbearance of those whose favourite churchyard has been omitted, whether it be through his choice or through his ignorance.

PART ONE

1. Burials through the ages

Although this chapter is primarily concerned with churchyards, whose main, though not sole purpose, was to provide facilities for disposing of the dead, it may not be inappropriate by way of introduction to make brief mention of earlier organised burials in Wales, for which there is sufficient surviving evidence, burials which in many cases predated by many centuries the sanctifying of Christian churchyards.

The earliest known burial places in Wales were in the New Stone Age, when, some time before 2000 BC, the dead were buried in specially constructed tombs, to which the name of long barrow is now given. A long barrow was a cemetery for a community because the neolithic people were farmers and therefore settled in one place. They dug passages in the ground, which they carefully shored up with large, upright stones, made burial chambers in the sides of the passages and roofed the whole grave over with huge capstones. When the community deemed the tomb to be full, soil was heaped up over it and the long barrow was closed. Excellent examples of such former communal burial places may be seen at Tinkinswood in Glamorgan, not very far west of Cardiff, at Pentre Ifan in the Pembrokeshire part of Dyfed, at Capel Garmon above the Conwy Valley in Gwynedd and at Bryn-celli-ddu and at Barclodiad y Gawres, both on the island of Anglesey. Occasionally, even as early as in the later part of the New Stone Age cremation was practised but probably not at the burial places just cited.

With the arrival shortly after 2000 BC of new tribes, whose culture was associated with the Bronze Age, the settled habits of their neolithic predecessors were for a while abandoned, as the new immigrants turned once more to nomadic habits. In consequence burials were usually of individuals, who were buried in the place where they had died, their bodies being placed either in pits dug in the ground or in slab-lined stone boxes, also in the ground. In both cases mounds of earth were

Bryn Celli Ddu, Anglesey

Capel Garmon, Conwy Valley
Prehistoric Burial Places

11

subsequently thrown over the bodies, thus creating round barrows, which were much smaller than the long barrows of the New Stone Age. By about 1500 BC inhumation seems to have given way generally to cremation. It must be emphasised that most of our knowledge of the way of life of the neolithic and Bronze Age peoples has been obtained from the careful study of the everyday artefacts, which were by custom buried with the dead.

By about 1000 BC, in the later stages of the Bronze Age, when changes were in the air, cremation had become universal; the ashes were placed in pottery urns, which unfortunately for archaeologists were not accompanied by artefacts. Five hundred years later still big changes materialised, with new races coming over here from the mainland of Europe. These newcomers were the Celts, the forerunners of true Welshmen, who ushered in the Iron Age. These new colonists came in three separate invasions, from three different locations but, wherever they came from, they paid no attention at all to burial rites and rituals. In consequence what we know about these early Celts is derived from the study of such things as their forts and their agricultural methods rather than from any study of their graves, which were anonymous and therefore rapidly unrecognisable as such. The Roman occupation of Wales, which began about 70 AD, was to overlap this long period of Celtic occupation, but of Roman burials in Wales there is little trace, save for occasional graves found in the Roman strongholds of Caerleon and Caer-went. In fact, there is no surviving record of any further burial in Wales until the spread of Christianity in the west in the late 5th century AD.

The first Christian burials in Wales were probably of Celts who had been won over to the new religion by zealous Christian missionaries who had come over either from Brittany or from Ireland less than a hundred years after the Roman withdrawal from Britain. These devoted men, once they had succeeded in making worth-while contacts in a locality, had to look for suitable places in which to build their simple huts; once these were built, they put up wooden crosses nearby, around which their services were held and around which in the fullness of time were dug the graves of early Christians. This setting of hut, cross and graves marked the very first llans, the first pieces of land set apart and sanctified for Christian usage.

In the course of the sixth and seventh centuries, these burial grounds became churchyards, as permanent religious structures took the place of the flimsy huts of the first missionaries. There are still to be seen in Wales very many circular churchyards, some of which may well have been in constant use since the early days of Christian settlement. In Powys alone there are still more than seventy round churchyards, of which most are to be found in what used to be known as Radnorshire. The first missionaries, as they sought suitable sites, looked for protection as well as assured supplies of water. Hence surviving prehistoric sites, particularly those of the Bronze Age, which were already protected by circular banks, tended to attract the attention of Christian settlers, especially when there were wells there too.

Students today are recommended to look carefully at the shapes of the churchyards they are studying, ignoring the age of the churches, which in most instances bear no relation to the age of the sites. If the churchyard is both round and raised up, the likelihood is that the site is an ancient one. Between the fifth and the eighth centuries the missionaries did their great work of evangelisation, Christianising most of Wales; at the beginning of the seventh century there had arisen a real chance of Christian reunion between the Welsh and the English churches, which had gone their separate ways in the dark days after the Roman withdrawal from Britain at the beginning of the fifth century. In 602 Augustine, who had a few years previously been sent from Rome to re-establish the Christian church in eastern Britain, summoned representatives of this Welsh church to meet him at Aust, just south of the Bristol Channel. The subsequent failure of this historic meeting to achieve unity, responsibility for which must at least in part be cited as being due to the Archbishop's intransigence, meant that the two churches continued to draw apart, as they went their different ways. Gradually and inexorably however the power of Canterbury prevailed with the result that the pattern of English diocesan and parochial organisation was eventually imposed upon Wales, a pattern that was only broken when the Church was disestablished in Wales in 1920.

Throughout the Middle Ages the churchyard was to be the village meeting place: it should be noted that rarely did a church stand in the middle of a churchyard. Normally it was sited nearer the north boundary of the churchyard than the south. The larger, southern part was consecrated and became the place for burials, though in the centuries that elapsed before this part of the churchyard was completely filled with graves, it was to be used for a number of secular activities that might strike us today as being unsuitable for sanctified ground. The smaller, northern part, however, remained unconsecrated throughout the Middle Ages; this was where the men, women and children of the parish came to spend their leisure hours. Certainly games were played there, (in Wales, all manner of games continued to be indulged in in the churchyard for a much longer period than they were in England, enduring in some parts, especially in the Radnorshire part of Powys, well into the nineteenth century), markets too were sometimes held there and plays performed. In addition patronal feasts were celebrated there — and noisily, too — while dancing and drinking ale were frequent pastimes. When the weather interfered with the enjoyment of these secular activities, they were normally transferred to the nave of the church, which, like the north side of the churchyard, remained unconsecrated in the Middle Ages. It has also to be admitted that even cock-fighting, that most barbarous of sports, not only sometimes took place in the churchyard but also occasionally was tolerated in the nave. This unconsecrated north part of the churchyard was also used on occasion, with or without official sanction, to afford burial to those who had fallen foul of the laws of God or man.

In the sixteenth century, the time of the Reformation and the Renaissance, which followed the Middle Ages, the social importance of the church and churchyard, in Wales as in England, had become somewhat diminished. To start with, the group awareness of medieval times, which had made the men and women of the parish willingly undertake duties and responsibilities, had given place to individualism; in addition, central government had begun to make itself responsible for

14

some of the tasks, which hitherto had been performed by officials of the parish, of whom the churchwardens were far and away the most influential. In the first half of the next century, the seventeenth, the country was torn asunder by civil strife, which for a time weakened and threatened the very fabric of society. In the years of intermission, during the Commonwealth in the 1650s, religious divisions were allowed to come to the surface, enabling those who refused to conform for the first time to assert themselves and to begin to spread their wings. Thirty years later, thanks to the Toleration Act of 1689, which was an essential part of the Revolution Settlement, Christians who had broken away from the Established Church, were allowed, provided that they were not Roman Catholics, at last to worship in churches of their own choosing. Before very long in Wales the Methodist Revival came about, with Daniel Rowland, William Williams and above all Hywel Harris on call to lead and organise. Even before the passage of the Toleration Act the Society of Friends, whom their enemies dubbed Quakers, had been quietly gaining strength in Wales.

In the eighteenth century the fire seemed to go out of religious enthusiasm, the zeal of the previous century being quenched by widespread indifference. In consequence many churches fell into almost total disrepair and many untended churchyards reverted to their natural condition. Happily in the nineteenth century there was much new building and even more rebuilding as the Victorians gradually became devoted to church attendance. As the population was rapidly expanding at the same time, very often the north side of the churchyard had to be consecrated to provide extra burial space, as no further burials were possible in the overcrowded southern side. This pressure on burial space however later became relaxed partly because of the creation of undenominational cemeteries, as opposed to churchyards, which catered only for the needs of members of the Established Church, partly because nonconformist chapels had their own burial grounds, and partly because of the adoption of cremation toward the end of the century.

Dr William Price, of Llantrisant in Glamorgan, a general practitioner, whose life seemed to consist of a marvellous succession of eccentric interludes, in 1883, when he was 83 years of age, horrified his neighbours by cremating the body of his infant son in a field near his home. These neighbours reported the matter to the police who arrested the doctor, who was brought to trial, where he conducted his own defence so skilfully that he won the day. In a historic judgment Mr Justice Stephen made cremation legal provided that no nuisance was thereby caused to others. So quickly has this idea of cremation been accepted that in our lifetime the pressure on churchyards has been for the most part eased. Today, very many churchyards have become peaceful but often untended places, where bird-life thrives and conservationists are enabled to study the flora and fauna. It would however be a pity if such churchyards became so overgrown that they were no longer recognisable as burial grounds at all.

2. Churchyards on prehistoric sites

In the last chapter the occasional use by Christian missionaries of earlier pagan Bronze Age sites was commented upon; this was seen to happen more often when a constant supply of water was confirmed by the presence of a well nearby. There was too another reason which is thought sometimes to have influenced early men in choosing to use an existing burial site, the desire to continue a tradition of burying in sacred ground. This sense of continuity of religious association, which in some early cultures was very strong indeed, may in part have been caused by the superstitious belief that there was such magical strength to be found in the protective circle, whether it was made of stone or of turves, that the spirits of the dead, be they pagan or Christian, might in some wonderful, incomprehensible way be preserved from any evil influences that operated outside the sacred circle. Some of these preChristian burial grounds, which were re-used by early Christians, also contained circles of yew trees, while in a few of them standing stones are still to be seen or sections of stone circles. More will be said in a later chapter about the significance of yew trees.

In Wales there are a great many Christian sites, dating from the sixth to the eighth centuries, which may well have been in use previously. An example of this, one among very many, can be seen at Meidrim in Dyfed (GR 289299), where, although there is no archaelogical proof of a Bronze Age settlement, the siting of the church certainly suggests one. It is built on top of a large mound and the extensive churchyard is circular, bounded by the edges of the very steep mound, which are marked out by more than thirty yew trees. A similar situation can be seen at Llanddwywe, on the west coast of Gwynedd, south of Llanbedr (GR 587234), where the present church stands in a raised round churchyard, which in prehistoric times was home for early men and women.

Of certain sites, eight have been selected for special comment because, in all these cases the connection with earlier times is clear and the continuity of religious association well established. Glasgwm, whose churchyard is the first to be visited, lies on a minor road in Powys, between the A481 and the B4594, (GR 157532). Today's settlement, as the village is approached from the east, consists of the old Rectory, the Post Office, a Youth Hostel, which was formerly the local school, and a collection of houses, four of which were inns a century ago. Beyond stands the parish church, which is very large indeed, beyond which is the last house in Glasgwm, originally known as the Yat. It was later raised by an aspiring squire to the social eminence of Glasgwm Court. In all Glasgwm today amounts only to a small village in a remote and very beautiful valley under the wild Radnorshire hills. Life once throbbed hereabouts but the tide of history ebbed and left it, as it is today, a quiet, largely forgotten and unassuming village, its name Glasgwm, telling something of its story, meaning the monastic community in the valley. The church is dedicated to St David, and many believe that David himself may have founded the first class here. Certainly in early days there was here a Christian monastic community, whose first simple buildings occupied the site on which the present medieval church stands. Although these early Celtic Christian missionaries established themselves here somewhere between the seventh and the tenth centuries, these devoted men were by no means the valley's first inhabitants because the church is built

17

upon the truncated top of a raised mound which was probably used as a burial place by men of the Bronze Age. This theory find some confirmation in the presence of a semi-circle of yew trees that runs round the west and south-west sides of the church. The church itself stands in a huge circular churchyard, which often indicates continuity of religious usage. Further evidence that Bronze Age people lived in these parts may be seen in the round barrow, known as the Giant's Grave, a mile or so the north-west of Glasgwm; this barrow is but one of many such Bronze Age burials to be seen in this neighbourhood.

A few miles north from Glasgwm over the hills on the A44 about two and a half miles south-west of New Radnor lies the small village of Llanfihangel Nant Melan, in beautiful and wild mountainous scenery. The main road runs through the village past the church which lies on the north side of the road, just past the hotel. As the name of the village and the dedication of the church suggest, St Michael made himself responsible for the welfare of the place, keeping it secure from the fearsome and unsleeping dragon, who was believed to wander at large on the Radnor Forest which broods over the settlement. From a non-religious point of view the churchyard here is of considerably greater interest than the church, which was virtually rebuilt in 1846, its builder Thomas Nicholson of Hereford, consciously imitating the Norman splendours of Kilpeck. Today's church, however, is merely the latest in a line of sacred buildings built on the same site, the first of which was likely to have been put up in the earliest days of Christian missions in Radnorshire. The first church, like the present one, stood inside a ring of yew trees, originally numbering twelve, of which eight have survived. Once again early Christians chose to settle in a place already made sacred by pagan men and women of the Bronze Age, who buried their dead in round barrows, which they surrounded with protective rings of yew trees. There are many other round barrows in this neighbourhood, most of them unexcavated. The whole settlement of Llanfihangel Nant Melan has been carved out of the southern flank of the dragon's home, the Radnor Forest.

Old Radnor is a hill village, about 5 miles west of Kington, just

Stone Alignments at Gwytherin

Twrog's Stone at Maentwrog

19

off the A44; its geographical situation is striking, more than 800 feet above sea level on a spur and with a commanding view of the solid mass of Radnor Forest to the north, which a thousand and more years ago provided a stout defence against Offa and those who came after him and ever since has offered a solid buttress against too much intrusion on the part of Homo Sapiens. Today Old Radnor, formerly the most important centre in this part of Radnorshire, visually amounts to little more than the church, a seventeenth century inn and a cluster of modern bungalows on the road below the church. A closer look will reveal that the huge church, which is surely one of the finest in the whole of Wales, stands on the top of a mound above what are certainly prehistoric earthworks. The first settlers here were men of the Bronze Age, of whose stay in these parts nothing at all is known beyond what may be surmised from the study of this unexcavated burial mound. Early Christians moved in, possibly as early as in the sixth or seventh centuries, choosing a site, already made use of in prehistoric times, the circular churchyard furnishing extra proof of this continuity of usage.

Just inside the church is a plain old font, which is far and away the oldest object in the church, bridging the gap between prehistory and historical time. For, although it will in all probability have served as a font in the earliest Christian building on the site, its even earlier history is shrouded in the mists of time. Geologically it is an erratic boulder but early man called it into use for purposes now unknown to us. Stone monuments of early man abound in this neighbourhood and there is no proof from which group of stones Old Radnor's font was taken but a group of four standing stones known as The Four Stones (GR 245607) shows a clear gap where a fifth stone may once have stood. Local tradition assigns the font to this monument, still to be seen, on the road from Kinnerton to Walton.

Further evidence of the early Christian taking over for their own purposes of a prehistoric site can be seen in north Radnorshire, some three and a half miles south of Rhaeadr (*Rhayader*), in the parish churchyard of Llanwrthwl, a village situated virtually in a layby off the A483, which runs from Llandrindod Wells to Rhaeadr. As the visitor draws near to the south porch of the church, he will almost collide with a very large standing stone, which practically touches the church. The early Christian missionary, to whom the church is dedicated and after whom the village is named, was Gwyrthwl. If the report be true that he did his sixth century evangelising in this place, he must be credited with having deliberately chosen to make use of a site, previously used by the people of the Bronze Age, who left behind them many other monuments of their settlement on the hills around here. The eye of the imagination sees the Celtic monk creating his llan in this place by putting up a cross within sight of the massive stone, near which the church now stands. The fact that today's churchyard is raised up increases the likelihood that Bronze Age people actually lived on the site, though what the stone signifies is not known, unless it was to act as a marker to indicate where the dead were buried. The early Christian converts, gathering around their cross, will have been very much aware of the presence in their midst of earlier human settlers who cannot have lived less than a thousand years before them.

There is a similar story to be told about the village churchyard in Maentwrog in the Vale of Ffestiniog, a few miles inland from Harlech; the very name of the place means "the stone of Twrog", but who exactly Twrog was is by no means certain. Local folklore has it that Twrog was a giant who cast the huge stone from the sky to fall where it now almost touches the south porch of the parish church. A more likely explanation is that this was the same Twrog who gave his name to the village of Llandwrog, which lies four miles the Pwllheli side of Caernarfon. This Twrog was believed to be a Christian missionary who lived in the second half of the sixth century; he is credited with having consecrated a llan in Llandwrog and again in all probability another one at Maentwrog, where, as at Llanwrthwl, full advantage was taken of the existence of this stone, which was already held in veneration by those who lived there. Once again early Christians wisely built upon existing traditions, as they were bidden so to do by their masters in Rome. The presence quite near this stone of a number of very ancient and massive yew trees gives added belief to the theory that this place was a Bronze Age settlement, which early Christian worshippers in this llan would have known about.

This Christian missionary, Twrog, is believed to have died in 610.

Up and down Wales circumstantial evidence points to the probability of many early llans being deliberately consecrated on known pagan sites but firm facts are, not surprisingly, hard to come by. However three more instances will be given in this chapter where there is still visual proof of early non-Christian activity in places, later to be used by Christians. In the churchyard at Corwen on the A5 in North Wales once again a Christian llan was consecrated near a pagan stone and once again in later years a Christian church was built very near this stone, which however in Corwen's case is no longer as obvious as it still is at Llanwrthwl and at Maentwrog. When centuries later a porch was required for the church it was built around the existing stone. As the inside wall of the porch was subsequently plastered over, today's worshipper is unaware of this link with the remote past, though the stone is still clearly visible from the churchyard.

In a remote valley under the Denbighshire moors is the delightful village of Gwytherin where the church has been recently reconsecrated. The place presents a fascinating problem, as befits an area chosen by Ellis Peters (Edith Pargeter) for the setting of her medieval thriller, *A Morbid Taste for Bones*. The known facts are these. The church is dedicated to St Winifred, who, tradition asserts, was abbess of a convent here in the seventh century, after her miraculous restoration to life in Holywell by her famous uncle Beuno! It stands on a small rounded hill, its churchyard is circular and abounds in large and very old yew trees. Between the north wall of the church and the churchyard wall stand four stones, each about three feet high, regularly spaced at intervals of about six feet, on one of which there is a Latin inscription to the memory of one Vinnemaglus, the son of Senemaglus. One authority describes the stones as being fifth or sixth century memorial stones, erected to mark the graves of early Christians, one of whom is named, while another authority cites the stones as being of probable prehistoric origin.

To the writer of this book the probable solution seems to be that in the Bronze Age there was a settlement here on the hill, to which the four remaining stones bear witness. However it is known that very many centuries later, in the sixth century AD, an early Christian connection was established here, the present churchyard being in all probability consecrated as a llan, in which in the fullness of time Christians were buried, one of whom, presumably deemed worthy of special mention, had his name carved on one of these visual reminders of a much earlier way of life. Whether this reading of the past is true or false, few who visit Gwytherin will disagree with the view that it is a very special place. The best example of a churchyard being deliberately established on a prehistoric site is to be seen in the north of Dyfed at Ysbyty Cynfyn, which will be dealt with in detail later in this book.

3. Roman Remains in Churchyards

This chapter will be short, its importance only marginal, but of some interest to those who like to see a continuing thread in history. Although it is certainly true that before a Roman Emperor embraced Christianity in Britain, two Roman soldiers had died for their Christian faith in Caerleon, there is no record of any Christian church in Roman Wales. The Roman withdrawal from Britain was complete by 410 but they had left Wales some twenty years previously; even so, there was only a short interval between the departure of the last Roman soldier and the arrival of the first Christian missionary from Brittany. (It must in this connection be stressed that while the rest of Britain reverted to paganism when the Romans left, further west, in Wales, the work of Christian missionaries both from Brittany and a little later from Ireland began in the early years of the fifth century.)

Here and there in Welsh churches are to be seen signs of a one-time Roman presence; for instance, a Roman stone from nearby Castell Collen may be seen in the church porch at Llanbadarn Fawr in Powys, a mile or so from Llandrindod Wells, and there is evidence of considerable Roman brickwork in the walls of the parish church at Llanfair-ar-y-bryn in Dyfed, which probably stands on the site of a Roman fort. In addition, it is tempting though unjustifiable to dwell upon the thirteenth century parish church in Caer-went in Gwent, which houses many Roman objects, dug up in this most exciting and pleasant of Roman towns.

Though the concentration of Roman power, both military and civil, was mostly in the south, it is in churchyards in the north that the two best examples are to be found of Roman occupation. However, first a short stop has to be made near the fort of Segontium, built on a hill to the south of Caernarfon. A little distance from today's Roman museum on the same Beddgelert road stands the parish church of Llanbeblig, in whose churchyard there survives a Roman altar.

Caerhun is a small village, situated about four and a half miles upriver from Conwy; it stands on the B5106, which links Conwy with Betws-y-coed on the west side of the river Conwy. The church and churchyard, however, lie about half a mile on the river side of the road, to be approached down a minor road, indicated by a finger-post. Today's churchyard, around St Mary's church, occupies the north-east corner of the Roman Kanovium. This small Roman fort, originally put up in 75 AD, played its part as a staging post in the opening-up of North Wales by the occupying power, based on Chester. Three years later Roman engineers went on to build Segontium, a mile south of modern Caernarfon, thus completing the east-west chain of forts.

Kanovium, which was rebuilt in stone in about 150 AD, was also intended to act as a strong point for dealing with attacks from the river, archaeologists, who from 1926-9 excavated the site, finding under the surface of the river signs of a jetty and a dock. It is not known at what date the first Christian church was built here (the oldest part of the present building dates from the thirteenth century), but it is at least known, thanks again to archaeological expertise, that the Roman site was not left entirely unoccupied after the Roman withdrawal at the end of the fourth century. Certainly there were squatters on the site in after years, either seeking such security as the Roman walls afforded or even perhaps living in what remained of the Roman buildings. Coins and pottery have been dug up to prove this later occupation. It is indeed just possible that the first Christians in

Caergybi, Anglesey — Roman tower in churchyard wall

*Caerhun, Conwy Valley — aerial photograph of church and churchyard
inside the Roman settlement (Kanovium).*

Caerhun may have been amongst these very squatters. What cannot be known, of course, is what archaeological evidence there is, still undiscovered under the surface of St Mary's churchyard, because the archaeologists, who dug the site in the 1920s, were not, of course, allowed to investigate the churchyard. Visual signs of the Roman fort at Caerhun today are limited to the south side and the SE corner of the churchyard walls which are still very obviously supported by Roman ramparts.

The last churchyard with Roman connections to be visited is strikingly situated on a hill, which overlooks the harbour in Holyhead, in the N.W. corner of Anglesey. Here St Cybi's church still stands inside the well-preserved walls of a Roman fort. When towards the end of the Roman occupation of Britain, all coasts were being threatened by barbarian invaders from various directions, here in Holyhead in about 300 a small fort was erected in an attempt to fend off any marauder from the sea. At the same time in east and south Britain numerous such forts were also being put up for the same desperate purpose along what came to be called the Saxon Shore.

Caer Gybi was contained by walls, which still stand over ten feet high and are five feet thick, with round towers in the angles, three of which survive. The useful life of this small Roman shore fort was a very short one, as the Romans had to leave the district in the same century that it was built. In the sixth century St Cybi, one of the early Christian missionaries, who probably hailed from Ireland, built the first Christian church in those parts, not surprisingly taking advantage of the protection of the strong Roman walls. Today a walk along those sturdy Roman ramparts, that still serve the church as churchyard walls, will strengthen a sense of historical continuity in all but the least imaginative visitors.

4. Holy Wells

In Wales, as has already been seen, many early llans were established on Bronze Age sites; the missionaries who had been successful in making local connections, when choosing the best place in which to build, had to look first for an abundant supply of water, with which for obvious reasons the Bronze Age settlements had been furnished. Such surviving wells were taken over by the Christian missionaries who blessed them and very often dedicated them to the Virgin Mary. Many a well had had a long and useful history before it was sanctified for Christian use. Former pagan wells, once they were blessed into holiness by Christian priests, acted as suppliers of holy water for the fonts of churches, which often shared the same dedication as the wells. Thus a Llanfair church often had a Ffynnon Fair in the churchyard or near at hand. It was no uncommon occurrence for priests to bless prehistoric megaliths as well as wells, especially if they were also, like the wells, in the neighbourhood of churches. Francis Jones, the acknowledged authority on wells, in his book *The Holy Wells of Wales*, cites in all more than a hundred pagan sites in Wales which were converted to Christian use by the rededication of wells and megaliths or by the erection of new churches near recently sanctified wells. Most of these wells were probably outside the actual churchyards, but were near enough to be thought within their spiritual ambit, as at Trelech in Gwent, where, despite its distance from the church, the well played a vital part in the life of the church.

Of the wells, which were consecrated in great numbers in Wales as early Christianity spread, many still survive, even if only in vestigial form. None is more celebrated than the one associated with St Winifred at Holywell (*Treffynnon*) in Clwyd. The unfortunate Winifred, the legend insists, was decapitated in the seventh century by a thwarted would-be rapist, a spring appearing where her severed head touched the ground. The fact that poor Winifred, thanks to the miraculous appearance and intervention of her famous uncle, Beuno, was speedily restored to life and full health, adds a bizarre touch to the story. The healing qualities of St Winifred's Well became such that a great cult developed over the years, a cult that shows little sign of diminishing in the twentieth century.

Very many wells retained into modern times their reputations for curing the sick, many of whom would first bathe in the well and then, where there was a prehistoric cromlech conveniently close, they would be carried there to lie in its shadow in the belief that a cure might thus be further hastened. In the nineteenth and early years of the twentieth century wells became popular as picnic sites; visitors who came to enjoy themselves, however, generally paid sufficient deference to ancient practice to continue to throw pins, (bent ones, if they wanted to put a curse on someone) into the wells, as their forbears had done. Particularly in central Wales there was a tradition that favoured dancing round the head of the well and drinking sugared water. In probably the last phase of their social usefulness many wells in country districts, provided that they were close to local churches, became popular venues for Sunday School treats, which sometimes took place on Trinity Sunday. There are, in addition, a number of churchyards in Wales, which still have within their boundaries wells, which once played significant roles in the lives of local communities. These wells are, of course, rare and as such should be treasured, perhaps rather more than is in all cases readily apparent.

Moving from north to south, the first such well to be described is in Anglesey, in the small village of Cerrig Ceinwen (GR 424738): though less than three miles from Anglesey's busy market town of Llangefni, the village has an attractive air of remoteness about it. The church is pleasantly situated in a dell, which is about fifteen feet lower than the road above, from which access to the churchyard is down a steep and winding path that goes near the well, which is on the south side of the churchyard. There is no marker at the site but in the neatly-maintained churchyard it stands out and is indeed quite active. Within living memory it had provided the local people with a plentiful supply of pure water, which not even in the severest drought had ever been known to fail. In addition, of course, generations of local children have been christened in the church at the font, which the well kept replenished.

Further south, but still in Gwynedd, in the Conwy Valley, is another churchyard well, the remotest in all Wales; to get there requires persistence and perseverance of a high order! This church at Llangelynnin (GR 752737) (which is not to be confused with another ancient church of the same name, also in Gwynedd,

Llangelynnin, Conwy Valley

Llangennith, Gower

on the coast between Dolgellau and Tywyn), dates from the thirteenth century and is 900 feet above sea level. An Ordnance Survey map is essential, and even that, though it gives the church a cross, fails to give it a name. As the crow flies and the walker scrambles, Llangelynnin is little more than a mile north of Ro-wen but it is necessary, if a car is being used, to proceed via the valley-bottom road B5106, leaving it about two miles south of Conwy, before taking to the narrow lanes — gingerly — and in an upward direction, map in hand! The car may be left, when the road runs out, near a farm which is a few hundred yards short of the church. Great is the reward for the faithful; the well which is in the southern corner of the churchyard, is well-preserved and walled around, except for a narrow entrance. There is seating accommodation at the side of the well, in the depths of which many a coin may still be seen. At one time it was roofed over; the well acquired a considerable reputation for curing the ills of sick children who lodged at a farm nearby. Also in the churchyard, but south of the church there was at one time a cock-pit.

Further east, in Clwyd, south-east of Holywell is Halkyn (*Helygain*, GR 209712); here in 1877 St Mary's church was taken down and a new church built on a new site just across the road from the former ancient churchyard. This original churchyard, today obscured from public view by a stone wall and tall trees, is well worth a diversion; it is extensive, circular and on raised ground, posing the usual query about the possibility of it having been a Bronze Age site. Near and under a circle of large and therefore ancient yew trees many gravestones, dating from the eighteenth century and the early years of the nineteenth, may still be seen and their inscriptions read. These graves are clustered around a grass-covered table-land, where the former church once stood; beyond this platform and the yews in the lower-lying south side of the churchyard may be found by the patient seeker a spring of water, bubbling up from the well, which supplied an earlier age with water, be these early inhabitants people of the Bronze Age or early Christian settlers there. After Christian sanctification the well provided for many years water for the font of the first church to be dedicated to St Mary on that site.

Less than ten miles west of Welshpool in old Montgomeryshire is the small town of Llanfair Caereinion, separated from the traffic of the A470 Welshpool to Dolgellau road by a bridge which spans the river Banwy. Like many Welsh place names Llanfair Caereinion is informative; its church is dedicated to St Mary and in former times there was some Roman fortification there, probably linked to the much more important Roman stronghold at Caersws. The church was built in the thirteenth century, on a hilly site, west of the town, above the river; the very large churchyard, from which many gravestones have been taken up and resited in preferred positions along the churchyard wall, possesses two unusual features; there is in its south-east corner a Presbyterian church (Welsh Methodist) which must bring pleasure to ecumenically-minded Christians, while on the north side of the churchyard, high up above the river Banw a stone path leads down to a well. This well, which has obviously had much care devoted to it over the years, seems likely to have served the needs of a local community here long before the thirteenth century, when it was Christianised and dedicated to the use of the newly-built church.

The A488 in Powys runs in a south-westerly direction from Knighton towards Llandrindod Wells; after four miles turn left on to the B4356, which opens up the beautiful valley of the Lugg, a tributary of the Wye. A mile along this road a finger post will be seen on the left hand side, pointing up the hillside to the as yet invisible Pilleth church (*Pyllalai*, GR 257683). There is no village to guide the traveller, only a rutted, grass-grown lane, which in about six hundred yards reveals a wide white gate, beyond which up a stately stone flight of steps stands on the hillside Pilleth church. A car can with care be manoeuvred up this lane, and there is a suitable place for reversing near the church, in whose well-tended churchyard, north-west of the church, will be found a well. The church was built in the thirteenth or fourteenth century and was dedicated to St Mary, in whose name the well was also sanctified. In the centuries that followed this well gained a considerable reputation for bringing relief to those troubled with diseases of the eye. This Lugg Valley had been much settled by men in the Bronze Age and it seems more than likely that this

31

well once served a Bronze Age community. It may also in the early years of the fifteenth century have slaked the thirsts of those unfortunate men who were caught up in a battle that was fought on the nearby hillside. For, in 1402 Rhys Gethin, lieutenant of Owain Glyndŵr, drew up his forces near the church, and proceeded to shoot their arrows with deadly accuracy down towards the valley along which an English army, led by Edmund Mortimer, was advancing. In the ensuing skirmish Mortimer lost a thousand men and the victorious Welsh took prisoner Mortimer, nephew of the future Edward IV. Today on the hillside, just above the church may be seen a clump of four redwoods, planted in a stone enclosure to mark the site of the battle that Shakespeare mentioned in *Henry IV* (Part 2).

While investigating the Gower Peninsula in search of churchyards, a necessary visit was made to Oxwich (GR 505862) on the south coast, in an area of outstanding prehistoric and historic interest. Would-be visitors to Oxwich church, who are unfamiliar with the district, are advised to go there out of season, as its holiday attractions result in the sort of congestion that hardly prepares the mind for the reflective attitude that such a remote and ancient place calls for. The church itself lies south-west of the village on the side of a cliff and has to be approached along a woodland path; it is small and secret, though the tower, presumably erected for defensive purposes, is immense. The church possesses an ancient font which, tradition asserts, was brought there by none other than St Illtud himself, to whom the church is dedicated. The churchyard on the landward side is very steep indeed and thus unsuitable for burials; hence the graves look as if they were huddled around the church. The underlying reason for a visit was to try to find the well in the churchyard, which in former times had been essential to those who lived there. After much vain searching a damp patch of ground was observed, that widened and eventually led to a sloping bank, above which a yew was bowing. Here, quite overgrown by ivy, was the well, which would have remained hidden from view but for a wet patch which was unexpected after so dry a summer as 1989 enjoyed.

In the middle of the maze of narrow roads to be found within

Ffynnon Non, St Davids

the triangle that bounds Fishguard, St Davids and Haverfordwest is the village of Llandeloy (*Llan-lwy*), GR 857267), in the centre of which, set back from the village street, stands the church, dedicated to St Teilo. The church itself is striking, representing a skilful attempt made in 1924 to reproduce an old Celtic church; the purpose of this visit, however, was once again to try to find the churchyard well of whose existence the village postmistress along the road was unaware. The grass in the churchyard had been carefully mown and there were few gravestones to obstruct the field of vision but of the well there was no sign until Freddie, who lived opposite the church, appeared, anxious to render any assistance required. He soon solved the problem by pointing to a region, covered by a very healthy bed of nettles, where the well was to be found, explaining that up to this year he had always, while mowing the grass, cleared the way to the well, whose merits as an unfailing source of pure water he was quick to praise. Soon it appears likely that the well will be hidden for ever, because the closure of the church is thought imminent, as church attendance has dropped to four.

It seems altogether fitting that this chapter which has concerned itself so much with matters of moment in the early days of the Christian church should end with a short pilgrimage to the area, made special by St David himself. One mile south of the city of St Davids in a field on a headland overlooking the sea may be seen the ruins of a chapel, dedicated to St Non, St David's mother, who, according to legend, gave birth to her son on that very spot. Although the ruins are of some interest, containing as they do a seventh century gravestone, special note should be taken of a number of low stones that stand up in the long grass of the chapel field, the existence of which suggests a former Bronze Age alignment there. Such a view seems strongly reinforced by the presence nearby of a well. Here then in all probability was a Bronze Age settlement, of which, of course, the well was an essential part; this well, Ffynnon Non, like so many others, was later Christianised and dedicated to St Mary, acquiring down the centuries a great reputation for healing all manner of diseases.

5. Early Christian Memorial Stones

Those who are interested in the whereabouts of the graves of early Christians in Wales owe an immense debt to the scholarship of Dr Nash-Williams, the author of *The Early Christian Monuments of Wales*. In this invaluable work of reference Nash-Williams catalogued all surviving Christian memorial stones in Wales, listing in all one hundred and thirty eight examples. He detailed their distribution and explained the origin of the Irish Ogham script, which appeared on some memorial stones in the fifth and sixth centuries, sometimes alongside Latin inscriptions and some times on their own. In the course of time many such early Christian grave markers were either destroyed or taken into churches or museums, or sometimes passed into private hands: It has to be remembered too that not all early Christian burials took place in churchyards, as some of those commemorated were buried where they died, on hillsides, at the side of the road, or, in one surviving instance in the Llŷn Peninsula, in what is now a farmyard. However, despite the changes that the years have brought, a number of such early gravestones may still be seen in situ, a selection of which now follows.

On all the very many fifth to seventh century Christian stones identified by Nash-Williams, there were certain distinctive Christian emblems, which ranged from a simple cross within an incised ring, unaccompanied by any verbal inscription, to named Chi-Rho burial stones, one of which is proudly exhibited in the church at Penmachno (GR 789506). HIC IACIT appeared on many stones (the grammatical HIC IACET rarely), as did the words IN PACE or PACE or even PA, along with the name of the person commemorated and often that of his or her father.

The location of a number of churchyards now follows, where Christian memorial stones survive in a recognisable form. The first one has already been described in another connection in Chapter 2; it is at Gwytherin under the Denbighshire moors in Clwyd where on the north side of the churchyard stands an alignment of four stones, the most easterly one of which commemorates Vinnemaglus. Three miles to the north of Gwytherin is the much busier village of Llangernyw, in whose raised circular churchyard there are two Christian stones, dated by Nash-Williams to the seventh to ninth centuries. The stones which are about six feet apart, stand very close to the south wall of the nave; on one an inscribed cross is quite clear but the surface of the other is obliterated by ivy.

Further west in Gwynedd, in the Llŷn Peninsula, more examples may be seen; under Tre'r Ceiri lies Llanaelhaearn, which is about six miles north of Pwllheli. Indeed there are two Christian memorial stones here, one of which, now in the church, was brought in from a nearby field where it was buried. The other stone still stands in the churchyard, just inside the gate to the right of the path that leads to the door of the church. It laconically remembers Melitus.

Llangïan is a village further west into the peninsula, about two miles north-west of Aber-soch. In the south side of the churchyard there, quite near the south door of the church, is a sixth century stone, which marks the grave of Melius, who was a doctor, the inscription reading "Melius, a doctor, the son of

Martin lies here". Little remote Llangïan provided a resting place for the first doctor known of in Wales. The stone has weathered badly and can only now be read in a good light. Some years ago a sun-dial was erected on top of it, which has now been removed, exposing the three holes through which the dial was once attached to the gravestone.

Much further south, in the most southerly part of Clwyd in the churchyard of the parish church of Llangedwyn, will be found, propped up against the east wall, a seventh to ninth century gravestone, in the head of which, enclosed in a circle, is a ringed cross; underneath this are five parallel vertical lines, which run down the stone to the ground. Further south again, this time in Powys, is the churchyard of St Cadog's, Llansbyddyd, situated on the south side of the A40, three miles west of Brecon; hidden in a mass of mostly untended nineteenth century graves on the north side is an unnamed memorial stone, identified by two circular ringed crosses, joined together by an incised stem. The higher of the two circles has four small circles around it. The churchyard is round, its periphery marked by ten ancient yews. Nash-Williams placed the date of the stone in the sixth century.

In Dyfed there are many churchyards, fortunate enough to have had entrusted to them early memorial stones, which survive. First to be commented upon is at Nevern (*Nanhyfer*) ten miles south-west of Cardigan, to which sheltered corner of south-west Wales an Irish monk, Brynach, is given the credit for having introduced Christianity in the sixth century. There are two sixth century named memorial stones to be seen here, one being in the church, where it acts as a window sill. It is inscribed to Maglicunus, the son of Clutorius, while the other one stands in the churchyard, near the south entrance to the church. It commemorates Vitalianus Emeretus, both in Latin and in Ogham, the Irish script which consists of stone incisions, arranged in groups from one to five lines.

North-east of Nevern, a mile or two south of Cardigan, is the sizeable village of Cilgerran (GR 191431), lying between A478 and A475. In the large churchyard, which was originally round but which has been extended in recent years, is to be found on the south side of the church in the middle of a row of nineteenth

Penmachno, Gwynedd

Cilgerran, Dyfed

Bridell, Dyfed

Cwmdu, Powys

century graves a sixth century memorial stone, engraved in Latin and in Ogham, the latter being much better preserved than the former, which can with some difficulty be made out to mark the grave of Tregenussus, the son of Macutrenus. Not far from Cilgerran, but back on the main road south to Tenby, the A478, is the hamlet of Bridell, (GR 176421) approximately three miles south of Cardigan; here above the road and to the west of it is St David's church, in whose churchyard is a towering fifth to sixth century memorial stone, about seven feet high, the very clear Ogham notches commemorating Nettasagrus; also on the slab is a cross, carved inside a circle, which is thought to have been added several centuries later. Three other memorial stones in this Pembrokeshire part of Dyfed in the churchyards at Pontfaen, Llanllawern and at St Dogwells (*Llantydewi*) will be described in more detail later in the book.

In addition, another six churches are recommended to visitors as in all of them will be found very early Christian memorial stones, which at one time or another were brought indoors from the adjacent churchyards. Pride of place must go to Penmachno church, which lies three miles south-west of the A5 in Gwynedd, between Pentrefoelas and Betws-y-coed. This church has in its safe keeping no fewer than four late fifth century or early sixth century stones of which the most remarkable is the one that bears the Chi-Rho monogram, remembering CARAUSIUS. One of the other three stones, all inscribed, was dug up in Penmachno churchyard when the present church was being rebuilt.

The other Chi-Rho inscribed stone in Wales is locked up in the little church of Treflys, (GR 532379) above Black Rock Sands near Porthmadog. This precious memorial stone, carved to remember IACONUS, the son of MINUS was found in the churchyard and wisely taken into the church. This Chi-Rho is not as clear an example as the one at Penmachno as it marks a transitional phase between the earlier Chi-Rho and a normal cross. Intending visitors are warned that the key to the church has to be obtained from the Rectory at Criccieth, five miles away.

The next two churches, trusted with the safe keeping of these rare treasures, are in Anglesey. Llangadwaladr (GR 383693) lies on the west side of the island, two miles east of Aberffraw, where the early kings of Gwynedd had their headquarters; one of these early rulers, a descendant of the founder of the dynasty, Cunedda was buried in the churchyard at Llangadwaladr. Today this memorial stone is in the church, built into the north wall. In some ways it is the most remarkable survival in Britain of early Christian times. This so-called Catamanus Stone commemorates "the wisest and the most famous of all kings, Catamanus".

The other Anglesey treasure-house is the church at Llansadwrn (GR 555759), in the south-east of the island, between Menai Bridge and Beaumaris; the church, which with the nearby farmhouse, seems to comprise today's community, looks after the tombstone, previously in the churchyard, of the founder of this church and his wife. The man is Sadwrn (Latinised in the inscription into Saturninus), who was none other than the brother of the great Illtud. The inscription reads: "Saturninus and his saintly wife lie buried here. Peace be with you both". This is the oldest such stone in Anglesey, as it is known that Sadwrn died in 530.

In central Wales in Powys, on the main road from Welshpool to Dolgellau is the village of Llanerfyl (GR 034098). Some years ago an early Christian grave was discovered underneath a huge and ancient yew in the churchyard. This inscribed stone, which now leans against the internal wall at the back of the nave, formerly marked the grave of a thirteen-year old Christian girl. "Here lies in this grave RUSTECE, daughter of Paterninus, aged thirteen years,. . . May she rest in peace".

There are a number of churches in Dyfed which have given shelter to inscribed stones, dug up in their churchyards, typical is the one to be seen in the church at Llanfihangel-ar-arth, a village, three miles east of Llandysul. The Eagle Inn, opposite the church, has custody of the church key. The church is built on top of a mound, suggesting the possibility of a pre-Christian settlement; it is fittingly dedicated to St Michael. The inscribed stone, now in the vestry, south of the chancel, recalls ULCAGNUS, the son of Senomaglus, who is believed to have died early in the sixth century.

6. Yew Trees

Every old churchyard in Wales probably possesses at least one yew tree; the trees may be old and gnarled, may perhaps have been reduced to stumps or may indeed have actually been cut down, though folk memory recalls the ominous consequences that follow such a savage undertaking. They are so much part and parcel of a churchyard that it ought to be relatively easy to account for their prevalence and their popularity in earlier times but the fact is however that, while many reasons have been advanced to explain their presence, there is absolutely no consensus of opinion on the matter, informed or otherwise.

It is known that yew trees had considerable significance in pre-Christian times, as they seem often to have been planted in Bronze Age burial sites. Why this was done is far from clear; some surmise that our prehistoric forebears chose to plant yews near their round barrows in the Bronze Age to indicate the presence in the neighbourhood of a plentiful supply of water. This theory, which was originally considered to be far-fetched, has in recent years received some confirmation from the findings of modern water diviners. Other believe that yew trees in early cultures were credited with the possession of magic properties. (It should be remembered here by cynics and scoffers that in the Middle Ages, when the authority of the Christian church in England was at its peak, magic wands were made of yew and the wood of yew was preferred by water diviners to that of hazel). As circles too were thought to possess supernatural properties, the bringing together of circles and yew trees may have been believed by prehistoric man to constitute a positive attempt to keep away evil spirits. The mind of early man was believed to have been much exercised by the activities of spirits, both good and bad, a belief that crystallised in the course of time into the division of the spirit world into that of God and the devil. Many of these dark fears and forebodings were to survive conversion to Christianity. As Christianity grew in popularity and more and more former pagans were persuaded to forgo their heathen ways and embrace Christianity, church leaders became increasingly worried by the widespread retention of pagan superstitions, which continued to flourish in their flocks. At length Rome itself was consulted on this matter and in consequence a firm instruction was sent to Christian missionaries in Britain to treat these surviving superstitions with patience and understanding, wherever possible allowing them to go uncorrected as long as no vital principle was involved. This advice from above may well have been interpreted by the worried missionaries and others to confer respectability upon the yew tree; it is interesting however to note that the Church was at the same time quite adamant in refusing to sanction the acceptance of mistletoe in Church.

That a yew tree was customarily planted near the church gate is confirmed by a reference in the twelfth century Book of Llandaf, where it was clearly stated that sanctuary would be available for "those who sought it between the yew tree and the church door." Furthermore clumps of yews sometimes provided useful temporary storage facilities for household goods in times of stress, when their owners were also claiming sanctuary either in the churchyard or in the church itself. In the Middle Ages farmers and landowners were expected to accept as part of their duties as members of a parish responsibility for maintaining the walls and fences of their churchyards. However it sometimes happened that their sense of duty took second place to their awareness of the excellence of the pasturing afforded by the lush unused parts of the churchyard. The less than adequate maintenance of some churchyard walls may well have been occasioned by this desire on the part of farmers to let their cows take advantage of the opportunities thus presented. Parish priests for their part sometimes reacted by planting yew trees at strategic points in these prospective pastures, knowing full well that the leaves of yew, though not the berries, as commonly believed, often proved fatal to cows. Churchyard walls had after all to be properly maintained and the Church regarded teaching as one of its proper activities!

Further encouragement for the cultivation of the yew was given by Edward 1st, when in 1307 he decreed that groups of yew trees should be planted in all churchyards in the land to provide some protection to the fabric of the church from high winds and gales. It is also generally believed, though not substantiated by documentary evidence, that another reason for the popularity of the tree in churchyards was the suitability of its wood for making bows. Certainly in an emergency — and life in the Middle Ages was full of local emergencies — many a bow was fashioned from local yew trees to fend off sudden attacks. Some caution is however necessary as the best yew for bows was imported from Spain and it is also known that the most successful bowmen in Wales, who lived in the south-east of the country, relied on bows made of elm rather than of yew. So very common were yews in the churchyards of Wales that on Ash Wednesday at the beginning of Lent the faithful, who wanted to show penitence, chose to smear their foreheads with ash, made from burning yew twigs, while later on in Lent, on Palm Sunday, if as so often happened there was no ready supply of hazel catkins available, recourse was generally had to sprigs of yew, plucked from the churchyard as worshippers entered church. Whatever the original reasons may have been for the presence of yews in holy places, it is perhaps significant that the evergreen nature of the tree made a wide appeal to Christians, who came to associate it with resurrection.

In the second part of this book, where a regional survey of churchyards is attempted, there will be found many references to yew trees in particular churchyards; suffice it here to draw the attention of the reader to a few other churchyards, not to be mentioned elsewhere in this book, where yews constitute an outstanding feature. In Montgomery, a delightful little Georgian town in Powys, there is a splendid avenue of yews, up above both sides of the sunken path that runs from the gate to the church door, while also in Powys, in the round and raised village churchyards of Llanfihangel Nant Melan and Llansantffraid-yn-Elfael, sections of circles of yews survive, indicating the likelihood of the sites having been used by men of the Bronze Age for round barrows. In Gwynedd, a few miles inland from Port Dinorwig (Y Felinheli), stands the isolated church of Llanddeiniolen, in whose churchyard are to be seen three of the largest and most gloomy yew trees in all Wales. Further east in Clwyd, north-east and south-east of Wrexham, are the respective and substantial village churches of Gresford and

Strata Florida, Dyfed — grave of Dafydd ap Gwilym

Llanfihangel Nant Melan, Powys

Overton; the yews in the latter are claimed to be among the Seven Wonders of Wales, as are the bells of the former, whose yew trees might also mount a similar challenge. The last word in this chapter must be reserved for one particular yew tree, that still grows in old Cardiganshire, now called Dyfed. Next to the former Cistercian abbey of Strata Florida is a churchyard, which now serves the adjacent parish church; here is the grave of one of Wales' foremost poets, Dafydd ap Gwilym. When he was buried here in the fourteenth century, Cistercian monks from the abbey planted on his grave a yew tree, which still flourishes and indeed dominates this modern churchyard.

7. The organisation of the churchyard

As many of the earliest churchyards in Wales back in the fifth or sixth centuries were set up in enclosures previously used by prehistoric people, their shape had been predetermined, but when new sites were required, the shape chosen was often circular, possibly in conscious imitation of surviving early churchyards. More detailed attention to the shape and organisation of churchyards probably did not become general until after the Norman conquest, when the parish system, which had had its roots in Saxon England, spread into Wales. That there are so many round churchyards in Wales is proof not only of the survival of very early settlements but also of the strength of local tradition in this matter. However, rectangular churchyards, which were usual on the mainland of Europe, became common in Wales too once the authority of the Archbishop of Canterbury succeeded in crossing Offa's Dyke.

Few, if any, medieval churches will be found in the very middle of a churchyard, the north side as a rule being considerably smaller than the south. This came about for a variety of reasons, the most cogent of which was that the south side was the only part of the churchyard to be consecrated. Seeing that most churches were built north of the settlement they served, the approach to the church porch was made through the larger south side where the sight of graves was deemed likely to make Christian worshippers, as they prepared themselves for service, to remember the dead and to pray for their souls, when they entered the church. Occasionally a church is found south of the village, in which case the normal arrangement was reversed and the church was built nearer to the south side of the churchyard than to the north. In the event it was the north side that was consecrated. This sometimes happened when the manor house had been built on the south side of the village.

It may surprise some readers to discover that only one part of the churchyard had been consecrated; in fact even within the church itself only the porch and the chancel were consecrated, one consequence of which was that the church authorities were only financially responsible for the maintenance of the chancel, the porch and the south side of the churchyard. The rest, the north side of the churchyard, the tower and the nave were the concern of the parish, whose representatives, the churchwardens, had somehow to find the necessary money to provide for the upkeep of these important but unconsecrated areas.

To provide decent burial for the dead was the prime use to which the south side of the churchyard was put, at the entrance to which stood the lych-gate (lych meaning corpse), where the priest met the funeral procession; it was here that the first part of the burial service took place. When in later years, in 1678, Parliament in its wisdom decided that all bodies should be buried in wool, the priest had an extra task to carry out at the lych-gate, namely to inspect the body to make sure that the law was being properly observed. After the initial acceptance of the body it was transferred to the parish bier and wheeled along the path through the south side of the churchyard to the south porch where the next part of the funeral was carried out. Many a rural Welsh church still has the parish bier at the back of the church or in the porch. Thereafter inside the church the main part of the service was held before the body was returned to the south side for interment. Here the body was carefully buried on its back with the head to the west so that it should face the rising sun; this age-old ritual probably stemmed from the sun worship. It is interesting to remember that in the early days of the Christian church in Britain the Pope countenanced the continuation of this ancient ritual in the hope that pagans might the more easily be converted to the Christian way.

In the course of the Middle Ages, when of course burials were confined to the south side of the churchyard, many churchyards faced a serious problem of overcrowding. Shrouded corpses were very often buried on top of each other, as the burial space was used up. In many areas the problem was solved by a periodic transference of some corpses to a charnel house, usually situated in a remote corner of the churchyard, where on All Hallow E'en the bones were burned to make room for the next intake. Where this rather unsavoury custom was not observed, the piling up of bodies continued, resulting in the general raising of the level of the south side, high up above the path that led from the lych gate to the church door.

In many a churchyard today may still be found evidence of crosses, sometimes a shaft, more often just the base, just occasionally the whole structure, which by some miracle escaped the implementation of the law; these crosses are usually on the south side and generally fairly close to the south door. While few of these date back further than to the fourteenth century, they often mark the places where in earlier times wooden crosses had been erected in the first llans in the springtime of the Christian religion in Wales. Thereafter the dead were buried round these marker crosses, even in some cases before the first proper churches were built. Two crosses, dating from much earlier than the fourteenth century, however, are well worth a special mention — and a special visit, one dating from the ninth century in the churchyard of St Canna's church at Llan-gan in Glamorgan, the other, a tenth century Celtic cross, adorns the churchyard of St Brynach's church at Nevern in south Dyfed.

Most of the crosses received rough treatment at the hands of Protestants at the time of the Reformation; many were smashed down to their very bases, while others that escaped this desecration were stumped to a height of four feet six inches in the next century, when Parliament decreed it. Other medieval crosses were preaching crosses, from the steps of which sermons were occasionally preached or the Gospel read on special occasions such as saints' days, Palm Sunday, Easter Sunday or at

Nevern Cross, Dyfed

Partrishow Cross, Powys

Trelech Cross, Gwent

Hanmer Cross, Clwyd

47

Whitsuntide. It is far from clear in some cases whether crosses are marker or preaching crosses, though some of the latter, erected rather later on, had small niches carved in the shafts for the safe custody of the pyx, which contained the host. Rarely there were in addition market crosses, even in the consecrated south side, a fact that many surprise some readers, but there was generally more room on the south side and anyway medieval man probably thought that higher standards of commercial morality might result from markets being held on consecrated ground.

All these crosses, whatever their original purpose, tended to be used for a variety of reasons, both religious and secular; for instance, it became the practice in later centuries for churchwardens to make public announcements from the steps of crosses on Sunday mornings after service. Even the crosses whose shafts had been reduced in size came in for a second life. In the middle ages vertical sundials had been scratched on the south walls of churches but by the sixteenth century a better way of telling the time had been found by having a horizontal sundial, for the securing of which the truncated crosses proved to be very suitable. Many a seventeenth or eighteenth century sundial is still visible attached to the top of a stumped medieval shaft.

Churchyards worth visiting for evidence of crosses of varying types, a very few of them whole, but all recognisable, include those at Llaneilian in Anglesey, at Derwen, Hanmer and Trelawnyd (*Newmarket*) in Clwyd, at Llanfilo, Cwm-du, and Partrishow (*Patrisio*) in Powys, at Bosherton in Dyfed, at Coychurch (*Llangrallo*), and at St Donats (*Sain Dunwyd*) and St Mary Hill (*Eglwys Fair y Mynydd*) in Glamorgan and at Grosmont in Gwent. There are of course a great many others beside, but should one cross only be selected for a pilgrimage, let the choice fall upon Partrishow.

In Wales, as in England, there were relatively few clocks in the Middle Ages, and most of these were in the big towns, the monasteries or in the country mansions; hence ordinary people had to depend on sundials to tell them the time. These had to be sited in a public place and the place most often chosen was the south side of the village church either on a wall or porch. Seeing that the desire to know the time was so general, it is surprising that so few of these medieval dials have survived in Wales, though this shortage is equally marked in many, though not all, parts of England. There must however surely be more than 4 such survivors in Wales, though the author is only familiar with those at Clynnog Fawr in Gwynedd, at Ewenni Priory, at Rhosili and at Llanddewi in Glamorgan. The most likely explanation for this state of affairs seems to be the widespread rebuilding and restoration of the outside walls of churches which took place in the eighteenth and early nineteenth centuries. Mention has already been made of the recall to use of the stumped shafts of churchyard crosses to hold horizontal sundials in the eighteenth century, while on one church tower in old Montgomeryshire at Tregynon a large sundial has taken the place of a clock.

On the north side of the churchyard in the Middle Ages the scene was a very different one from that on the south, because it was the village meeting place. Of the activities that went on there more will be said presently. Suffice it here to say that it was where friends met socially, where many different pastimes were pursued and where all and sundry naturally gathered for exercise of mind or body. Indeed it was an outdoor community centre and when the weather interrupted proceedings, all the various activities were transferred to the nave of the church, which, like the north side of the churchyard, remained unconsecrated during the Middle Ages.

Before dealing in some detail with these various activities, some mention must be made of occasional burials that took place on the north side. All parishioners, whether churchgoing or not, at death were deemed worthy of burial in consecrated ground except those who had taken the lives of others or — and this was felt to be almost as heinous a crime — had taken their own lives. These unfortunates were deprived of Christian burial but the bodies somehow had to be disposed of. They were sometimes buried, and often secretly at night, in a quiet corner of the north side. In medieval times no churchyard graves, either in the south or the north side, were named, so the unconsecrated graves were quite unmarked and presumably unrecognisable after a short time. Their very existence is known only from entries in the parish registers, where their names, crimes and dates of death were recorded, often accompanied by the stark comment "buried on the back side of the church".

In the Middle Ages religious plays, depicting scenes in the life of Christ and other Bible stories, were frequently performed in the naves of churches, the actors usually being the local priests, though from time to time suitable parishioners were chosen to take minor roles. Such scenes resembled visual accessories to sermons; the walls of the nave were generally covered with simple, colourful Biblical episodes, which helped to add life and meaning both to sermons and to religious plays. It has to be remembered that most members of congregations were probably quite illiterate and needed the help of pictures, both in spoken words and on the walls of the church. Nevertheless from time to time bishops frowned upon these simple dramas with the result that sometime in the thirteenth century they ordained that plays must no longer be performed in church. Instead they had in future to be acted in the churchyard; at about this time some trade guilds had begun to flourish and before long members of guilds often took over the acting of these religious plays from the clergy. In time these professional actors themselves left the churchyard, as they devised movable stages which they took with them to towns and villages.

The same bishops who were responsible for driving these plays into the churchyards were also opposed to the holding of markets in churchyards. At the end of the thirteenth century Edward 1st ordered markets not to be held on Sunday before a few years later ordering them out of the churchyard altogether. Of more significance perhaps was the more or less contemporary expulsion of fairs also from the churchyards, of more importance because there were far more fairs than markets. However, Wales was a very long way from London and this royal edict took all of three hundred years to reach all parts of the country! Fairs continued to flourish there until the end of the sixteenth century.

It has to be made clear that the medieval idea of a fair was very different indeed from ours; today the thought of a fair conjures up a picture of noise, bright lights and excitement. There may well have been much enjoyment in a medieval fair but its prime purpose was to encourage trade. If the reader thinks of a modern trade fair, a clearer picture will be gained of what went on in the medieval churchyard fair. Farmers and traders displayed their wares on trestle tables, while the supplementary needs of would-be purchasers were catered for by those who supplied food, drink and entertainment. These churchyard fairs made a real contribution to the life of the parish at a time when opportunities for social intercourse and exchange of ideas were severely limited. The church authorities too felt involved, as many fairs were linked to religious occasions such as saints' days.

Every church in former times once a year acknowledged the saint to which it was dedicated; this day of rejoicing involved much attention being paid to eating and drinking, which took place in the north side of the churchyard. In addition to secular enjoyment in the churchyard there was a service of thanksgiving in the church. Over the years a regular pattern emerged for the celebration of the patronal saint; on the eve of the feast a candle-lit procession formed up in the village before wending its way to the churchyard and into the church where a service was held. The following day, which was a public holiday, was celebrated with great enthusiasm in the churchyard, where all manner of games were played, with frequent adjournments to the trestle tables, which were well stocked with food and drink. It may well be imagined that sometimes secular enjoyment tended to obliterate the real purpose of the occasion, but all the same these patronal feasts did provide necessary opportunities for relaxation and enjoyment for very many simple parishoners. What in later years were called Parish Wakes were in most places merely the continuation of these early patronal celebrations.

In some parts however clearly excesses marred the celebrations from quite early times; indeed even in the twelfth century Giraldus Cambrensis painted a graphic picture of roistering teenagers on patronal eves leading the processions into the church, where they left their elders and the clergy to their prayers, while they congregated on the north side of the churchyard. Here they whirled away the night in noisy, drunken dancing. In many parts of Wales patronal celebrations, though it is to be hoped of a less riotous nature, went on, under their new guise of parish wakes, well into the second half of the nineteenth century.

This is no place for detailing the manifold activities of churchwardens in the heyday of the church in the Middle Ages beyond stressing above all else their onerous responsibility for raising enough money to pay for the maintenance of the community of which they were the senior welfare officers. The priest as representative of the church authorities paid only for the upkeep of the chancel and the south side of the churchyard; all else depended on the parish. In much later centuries a parish rate was necessarily applied but in the Middle Ages, although such an imposition was occasionally tried, it rarely proved successful and always stirred up resentment. The usual means chosen by the churchwarden to get money was to organise a church ale; at various times of the year as master of ceremonies he went round the farms, asking for gifts of malt, which was taken to the church-house, which was normally either very near the church or sometimes actually in the churchyard. Such a house was virtually the churchwarden's office; here helpers and volunteers, under the jurisdiction of the churchwarden, brewed as much strong ale as possible. A date was fixed and the ale took place on the north side of the churchyard, where tables and booths had been set up; all the parish was invited. There was as a rule a fixed tariff for the sale of ale, sensibly adjusted to local needs. Usually the unmarried paid an average sum, families paid rather less and visitors paid extra for the privilege of being there. There was too a well-established convention that the well-to-do had to make an extra contribution. The most popular ale of all was the one held at Whitsun, probably because there was at that time of year the least likelihood of bad weather necessitating the transfer of the festivities to the nave of the church. There were on occasions special ales organised for such special needs as the marriage of an orphan girl.

From time to time church ales were put at risk by episcopal displeasure and sometimes even by royal edict, but even an express prohibition by Henry VIII seems to have been for the most part ignored. The eating and drinking were generally followed by dancing in the churchyard to the accompaniment of pipes in some places, by flutes and violins in others. Meanwhile the young indulged in various games and pastimes, and not only, of course, during the church ales; indeed the church authorities encouraged these games, especially on Sunday afternoons, though in Clocaenog in Clwyd fives were generally played after service on Sunday morning. Fives was very popular, probably because the external walls of the tower and the north wall of the church, along with its buttresses, lent themselves to this particular ball game. At Llandyfalle, north of Brecon in Powys, iron hinges and iron stays may still be seen on the north wall, where they once held shutters, which protected the glass from the enthusiastic ball players. This north side of the churchyard, it must be remembered, was the village playground, the scene of many happy if noisy and occasionally over-boisterous pastimes, until the Methodist Revival came along to make an abrupt ending to most of the rollicking. This change in attitude is neatly summed up in the inscription which may be read in the church porch at Llanfair Isgoed (*Llanfair Disgoed*) in Gwent.

> Whoever hear on Sunday
> Will Practis Playing at Ball
> it May Be before Monday
> The Devil Will Have you All.

In the early autumn of 1989 it was removed for refurbishment, but apparently its speedy return is assured.

Though bodies were buried in the ground on the south side of the churchyard throughout the Middle Ages, there were no named memorial stones, no tributes in stone to the deceased, as there were inside the churches, in memory of those who by birth or achievement had acquired fame and reputation. Early in the seventeenth century, however, when the common man was beginning to rise a little in the world, memorial stones began to be erected outside in the churchyards; it is not perhaps surprising that the first such gravestones should represent a conscious imitation of the sort of memorial stones accorded to their social superiors inside the church. The very first named tombstones in the churchyard were flat horizontal slabs of stone, placed on top of the graves. This clearly was an attempt to reproduce outdoors the horizontal slabs which were familiar to all in the floors of medieval churches. It is worth noting that in the fullness of time these horizontal slabs in the churchyard tended to sink beyond recognition; when this was observed to be happening, these so called ledgers were raised up a little on to small stones to preserve them from oblivion. At about the same time too that these first horizontal ledgers were being placed over graves in the churchyard, short, thick vertical stones were sometimes being chosen by some; these were inserted in the ground at the east end of the grave, on which the appropriate details about the deceased were carved. These early outdoor gravestones whether horizontal or vertical, were probably the work of local handymen; in most areas it was not until the following century, the eighteenth, that specialised monumental masons, who up to then had concentrated on producing wall memorials inside churches, turned their attention to the churchyard, where now even the majority of the famous were being buried, as the unhealthy fashion of burying inside the churches came to an end. Thereafter the standard of gravestones considerably improved, as the vertical stones became less clumsy, thinner and higher. These memorial stones were more expertly carved and were often artistically embellished. The second half of the eighteenth century, and the nineteenth, were to become the golden years of the monumental masons.

8. Early Nonconformist Burial Grounds

Religious people who disagreed with the religious views of the Established Church, had their first chance in the seventeenth century to stand up and shout during the short-lived commonwealth that followed the abolition of the monarchy after the execution of Charles I in 1649. In those memorable years of change between 1649 and 1660 all manner of dissenting religious malcontents began to organise themselves into active, vocal groups; one of the most successful and historically important of these religious rebels was George Fox, who, virtually single-handed, founded the Quaker Movement. In the 1650s he visited Wales, with consequences for Radnorshire which will become apparent later in this chapter. In 1660, when the monarchy was restored and the previous status quo resumed, reaction set in with the passage of certain acts of parliament, commonly lumped together as the Clarendon Code, whereby all public expression of religious dissent was forbidden. Thereafter religious opposition was driven underground, where, of course it flourished. In 1689, as a part of the revolution settlement that accompanied the expulsion of James II and the accession of William III, Parliament passed the Toleration Act, which did away with the worst features of the Clarendon Code, assuring religious freedom to all Christians who would accept thirty-six of the thirty-nine articles of belief, insisted upon by the Church of England. In fact, even Roman Catholics and Unitarians, who refused to comply with the provisions of the Toleration Act, were generally ignored, when they broke the law, except in special circumstances, as in the Jacobite years of 1715 and 1745, when many Roman Catholics were regarded as politically suspect. After the seventeenth century new sects sprang up in Wales, mostly Independents and Baptists, and later in the century Presbyterians, who at that time in England were known as Methodists.

These Welsh dissenters needed burial grounds, as their dead were forbidden burial in consecrated ground in the existing churchyards of the church. George Fox, the founder of the Quaker Movement, who visited Wales several times, in 1657 preached outdoors on Pen-y-bont Common in Radnorshire, where he stood on a chair and for three hours addressed a large assembly of local people, many of whom had to sit patiently on horseback. The movement spread rapidly thereafter in Radnorshire, converted Quakers holding services in their own homes. Burial presented problems to them because the intolerance of the age prevented Quakers — and other dissenters — from being buried in consecrated ground. In 1673 a local farmer, who had heard Fox preach on that memorable occasion on Pen-y-bont Common sixteen years before, died, leaving money in his will for the purchase of a piece of land to be used as a Quaker burial ground. This piece of land, which was only two miles away from where Fox had preached, became the first

Quaker burial ground in Wales. In 1717 a further piece of land was bought adjoining the burial ground, where a Meeting House was duly built. The Pales Meeting House and burial ground near Llandegley (*Llandeglan*) are still in use. (GR 138641).

The burial ground is on an exciting site, carved out of the side of the Radnor forest at a height of eleven hundred feet; unfortunately there are no surviving written records of the early burials there and in addition Quaker graves were unmarked until the 1830s. However just over 70 headstones remain, the earliest of which bears the date 1838. All the nineteenth and most of the twentieth century gravestones carry only the barest description, such as JOHN JONES DIED ON THE 12th DAY OF THE 7th MONTH 1853, AGED 65 YEARS. A little gate separates the burial ground from the forecourt of the modest thatched meeting house, which is divided into two parts. In the room to the right services take place in surroundings that have changed very little in the past two hundred and seventy years. Some of the furnishings indeed are as old as the house. The room next door, separated from it by a screen, was once a school room, where in 1867 a day school for Quaker children was founded. The first headmaster was a Yorkshireman, William Knowles, whose stipend was a modest £50 a year. Originally there were twenty-five children on the roll, but the number doubled as the school's reputation grew. The venture came to an end in 1884, by which time a village school had been opened down below in Llandegley. An account of the story of the school is available in the former schoolroom, along with other literature of the Society of Friends, which will be found on top of a hand bier, which serves as a table. A visit to the Pales is an uplifting experience for many people; the simplicity of the place, along with the splendour of the panoramic view, brings to many its own special balm.

Less than ten miles from the Pales, as the buzzard flies, though considerably further as the motor-car finds its tortuous way through narrow Radnorshire lanes is Glasgwm, the outstanding features of whose early history were described in Chapter 2. One day in May 1871, Kilvert visited Glasgwm, having walked over the hills from Cleirwy (*Clyro*); he had an appointment with the

The Pales, Llandegley, Powys (Quaker)

Maes-yr-onnen, Powys (Independent)

57

vicar, whose ruddy face, white hair, merry eyes and authoritative manner much impressed the diarist. In this entry Kilvert mentioned the local squire, Beavan. He commented thus: "Just outside the churchyard the Beavan family have a private burial ground, unconsecrated, where a number of them are buried." In this matter, as in other matters connected with dissenters, Kilvert was misinformed. The truth is that in the eighteenth century there had been a strong Baptist connection in the Glasgwm area; their leader, a farmer, named John Lewis held services in his own house and when he died, made provision in his will for the purchase of a piece of land, opposite the churchyard, but separated from it by the main road, to be used as a Baptist burial ground. John Lewis himself was the first person to be buried there, his moss-covered grave, once cleared of Nature's encroachment, revealing his death in 1811 at the age of 72. Kilvert however, despite his known anti-dissenter prejudice, can be excused his mistake because by 1871, when he visited Glasgwm, the Beavan family, who had turned the nearby Yat into Glasgwm Court, seem to have taken over the burial ground. The burial ground today is quite untended and without an occasional visit with a suitable tool would in a short time become as forgotten as it is now forsaken. Recent scratching about has revealed that there are five Beavan table tombs there, in varying degrees of decay but on the ground almost completely obscured by moss and lichen are the graves of seven or eight Baptists, who died in the early years of the nineteenth century, John Lewis' grave being the one nearest to the road.

Further south, but still in Powys, the A438 Hereford to Brecon Road, after passing through Willersley runs in a south-westerly direction, just north of the river Wye; between Llowes and Glasbury, a right-hand turning off the A438 up a minor, hilly road leads after about half a mile to the Independent chapel and burial ground at Maes-yr-Onnen (GR 177411). This was one of the very first nonconformist chapels in Wales, having been consecrated in 1696. The building, which is much older, is thought to have been put up in the sixteenth century, when it was a farm and barn. The fittings and the furniture speak of the eighteenth and nineteenth centuries and indeed a visit to

Maes-yr-Onnen helps to impart a vivid sense of Welsh nonconformity in the last two centuries. Behind the chapel which is still in use as a place of worship, is a well-kept burial-ground, dating from 1822. There are more than thirty tombstones, of which the earliest commemorates a burial in 1838. The geographical position of Maes-yr-Onnen is as striking as that of the Quaker Meeting-house, already mentioned at the Pales, Llandegley, while the chapel itself, in the words of Jan Morris, "still breathes a spirit of elated discovery."

Soar-y-mynydd (GR 784533), the next place to be visited in this search for early nonconformist burial grounds, will only be seen by those who welcome the challenge of trying to find what has been called the remotest place of worship in the British Isles. The southern Cambrian Mountains, that separate the spas of Central Wales, Llandrindod, Builth and Llanwrtyd from the Tregaron and Lampeter area on the westward side are crossed by an adventurous road that links Llanwrtyd with Tregaron over the Abergwesyn Pass and up the Devil's Staircase. Soar Chapel is to be found about five miles along a minor road, which moves south from this mountainous route at GR 763567. The Ordnance Survey map, an essential companion on this journey, marks the track and the chapel, though only with a cross. Chief credit for the setting-up of this chapel must go to the father and organiser of Welsh Methodism, Hywel Harris, who, despite his life-long loyalty to the established church in his native Talgarth, yet inspired and organised and trained others so successfully that the independent Calvinist Methodist (Presbyterian) church in Wales grew out of his missionary work and started its separate and successful existence early in the nineteenth century. Apparently Harris as early as in 1740 came across from Talgarth and preached in a farm-house, not far from where Soar Chapel now stands, with such enthusiasm and missionary zeal that the seeds were sown which were to germinate in fertile soil and eventually led to the building and consecration of this independent chapel at Soar in 1822. Adjoining the chapel is a house, where the visiting preachers stayed the night and in front of it is the burial ground, below which is a grove of trees, which must do something to temper the edge of winds from the east. Services are still occasionally held and are exceptionally well-attended. In the burial ground stone stumps show up in the long grass, marking the graves of about twenty people, but of them only three are any longer legible. They relate to burials between 1830 and 1860.

The last burial place to be mentioned in this chapter is in the Llŷn Peninsula in Gwynedd, and although it is by no means as remote as Soar Chapel, it is still far from easy to come upon. The Grid Reference for Nanhoron Independent Chapel is 287309; it is less than three miles north-west of Aber-soch and not much more than a mile from the village of Nanhoron. The nearest house has a notice in the garden, with the welcome information that the key to the chapel may be obtained there and that the chapel lies two hundred yards up the green track at the side of the house. The lane is safe for a car which is just as well as two hundred yards seems something of an understatement! Would-be visitors must be ready to leave their cars where the lane bifurcates. Keep straight on and after a few yards a gap in the hedge on the right hand side reveals the chapel, separated from the lane by sturdy brambles, whose luscious fruit in September compensates for the diversion. Once inside the chapel (remember to insert the heavy key upside down!) the twentieth century fades away, as the original roughly-hewn wooden pews come into view, set in an uneven, earthen floor. In October 1769 the Justices of the Peace of Caernarfonshire licensed Nanhoron as an independent place of worship; its three founders were local men of considerable substance. A hand bier stands at the back of the chapel, beyond which in the extremely lush vegetation of the burial ground eight graves may still be recognised as such, the earliest recording a burial in 1821, the latest in 1862. All in all, Nanhoron is locked in a time warp.

Soar-y-mynydd, Dyfed (Methodist)

PART TWO

A REGIONAL SURVEY

1. GWYNEDD AND CLWYD

A. Anglesey (*Ynys Môn*)

It is generally believed that the Roman occupation of Wales ended shortly before the end of the fourth century AD, when the Emperor Maximus Magnus, known to the Welsh as Macsen Wledig, (he married the Welsh Helen) marched out from Caernarfon with his army when military necessity demanded his presence elsewhere in the Roman Empire. At about the same time, either by Roman invitation or by coincidence a Celtic chieftain, Cunedda came down with his fighting men from the Firth of Forth area of Strathclyde and set up his headquarters at Aberffraw in the west of Anglesey, where he proceeded to establish himself so successfully that his descendants were able to consolidate and expand their power base very considerably. Cunedda, though probably a Christian, took up arms against Irish settlers in Anglesey, many of whom were likewise Christian. The rivalry was finally resolved in about 500 AD by Cunedda's grandson, Cadwallon, who defeated the Irish in a decisive battle at Cerrig y Gwyddyl, near Trefdraeth. Fascinating evidence of the strength of Christianity in Anglesey at this time is provided by the survival of eleven Christian memorial stones, all dating from the sixth or seventh centuries and all bearing inscriptions either in Latin or in the Ogham script, which the Irish settlers invented. The church at Penrhos Llugwy (GR 481859) in east Anglesey, a mile or two inland from Moelfre, plays host to a sixth century memorial stone to an Irish chieftain; although the church is locked, the windows contain clear glass and it is possible to see the visual proof of continuing Irish influence in the sixth century.

Christian missionaries in Anglesey, particularly in the sixth

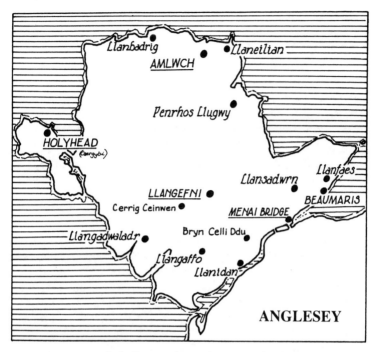

century, set up their llans, where they preached and talked so
persuasively that by the middle of that century three monasteries
(clasau) had been established, one at Holyhead, where St Cybi
built his clas inside the protective walls of the former Roman
fort, another at Penmon, where St Cybi's friend, St Seiriol
established himself and the third at Llansadwrn, north of Menai
Bridge and west of Beaumaris, where St Sadwrn, the brother of
St Illtud, taught and died (his memorial stone survives and is to
be seen today inside the parish church of Llansadwrn, where he
shares an inscription with his wife). It is the oldest Christian
memorial stone in Anglesey, dating from about 530. It has to be
pointed out that the title of saint is an honorary one, in this
context, as only St David was actually canonized by Rome.
Thereafter Christianity seems to have flourished with the
building of simple wooden churches in many parts of the island;
none of them, of course, survive, but happily their sites were very
sensibly used again and again for the building of sturdier

churches. Many a plain and unadorned Welsh church in Anglesey today was built in the nineteenth century but in a churchyard hallowed by the presence there more than a thousand years previously of early Christian missionaries.

In the ninth century, disaster struck Anglesey when the fearsome men from the north, the Vikings, who were in the process of conquering Ireland, made their first raid on the island in 844. For the next one hundred and fifty years, the Vikings lorded it in Ireland, and as long as they were ensconced there, Anglesey knew no peace, being invaded on no fewer than seven occasions. They felt the full force of the Viking fury for the last time in 987. Troubled times still lay ahead because in the following century the Normans made themselves masters of England, trying forty years later, albeit unsuccessfully, to make a foothold in Anglesey. Two hundred years elapsed before the Normans, by then accepted as the English, built Beaumaris Castle and garrisoned it with English soldiery.

The choice of particular churchyards to be included on our visiting list is invidious; however Anglesey is a small island and the churchyards selected are so sited geographically that many others may also be looked at without too much difficulty. Elsewhere in this book mention has already been made of Caergybi, Llansadwrn, Penrhos, Llugwy and Cerrig Ceinwen. First on this list is Llangadwaladr, (GR 383693); the churchyard is very extensive, much of it quite modern but it is a very ancient Christian site indeed, as in the early years, when Cunedda came down from Strathclyde after the Roman withdrawal, and settled in Aberffraw, here at Llangadwaladr, which is only two miles to the east of Aberffraw, the churchyard became the royal burial ground. The Catamanus Stone, dating from 625, which has already been referred to, was centuries ago dug up in the churchyard, which presumably still contains the graves of other early rulers who gradually extended their authority south until it reached the mouth of the river Teifi, where modern Cardigan stands. Llangadwaladr is the Frogmore of Gwynedd.

Llangaffo (GR 444683) is a large village, strung out along the road that runs north-eastwards from Newborough on the B4421. The churchyard here is unusual in several respects; to start with,

Llanfaes

the older graves are north of the church, the more modern ones south of it, indicating that the north side of the churchyard was consecrated first, the south side later, when pressure grew on burial space. Despite the very large number of graves in the churchyard, there is still considerable open space. Furthermore, between the road and the church, there is a large mound, which has resulted in the path to the church being sunken. Usually such a sunken approach shows the consequence of burying the dead on top of each other, as they did in the Middle Ages (when all burials in the churchyard were anonymous). However, such an explanation, though it may be in part valid, certainly cannot altogether account for the mound. One theory is that the church and churchyard were sited in a Bronze Age settlement, though in the absence of archaeological proof, no more than surmise is permissible. On the top of the mound there is a twentieth century war memorial and nearby the base and truncated shaft of a medieval cross. The mound is shored up on the church side by a low retaining wall, propped up against which are five early Christian grave-stones, all with crosses carved on them. To add further to the puzzle of the mound, in the nineteenth century a number of further burials took place there, to which well-preserved table tombs bear witness.

A mile south-east of Brynsiencyn (on the A4080) and almost on the shore of the Menai Strait a llan was established early in the seventh century by St Nidan, a pupil of St Kentigern, who was one of the early band of Christian missionaries who came down from Strathclyde. St Nidan chose for his llan a very sheltered site, hidden from the Menai Strait, but accessible from it. This settlement, which came to be known as Llanidan (GR 495669) saw over the centuries a succession of churches built on the original site, the latest of which was put up in the fourteenth century, which now unfortunately is a ruin. A pilgrimage undertaken to this churchyard is rewarding; there is little to distract and much to suggest the quiet years of Nidan's ministry in this secluded spot. In the spring the churchyard is carpeted with wild garlic. Some stillness still remains in secret places like Llanidan.

In the north-east corner of Anglesey is to be found one of the earliest Christian sites on the island and one of its most famous churches. Llaneilian (GR 478894) lies two miles east of Amlwch; sometime in the sixth century, according to legend, a Celtic missionary, St Eilian, landed on the rocky shore with his family and domestic animals, and proceeded to set up a llan there, where he acquired a reputation for converting the pagans and healing their sick. Essential for the success of such a mission was a plentiful supply of water near at hand; this was supplied by a well which today can with some difficulty be located some little distance from the church on privately-owned farm land. In later centuries, people came from far and wide, especially on the patronal day of the saint, January 13th, to drink from the well before going into the church to pray to the saint. So successful was St Eilian in making a Christian connection here that a number of churches were built on the site of the first llan; today's church was mostly put up in the fifteenth century, though it incorporated a stone tower and spire from the earlier church of the twelfth century and the fourteenth century chancel, from which a stone passage was later added which linked it with a mortuary chapel, known as St Eilian's Chapel, where a wooden shrine may still be seen. The great glory of the church is the magnificence of the carving in oak.

Outside the south porch are the solid steps of a medieval preaching cross, five feet of whose shaft still points to Heaven. The churchyard is very large and much overgrown, in summer time becoming almost impenetrable in places. The farmer, whose land adjoins the churchyard, told the author that when many years ago he first moved to this farm, on whose land the well was situated, he used the water for his cattle. Later he sought authorisation from the Ministry of Agriculture, who sent down an expert to take a sample. Many months elapsed before the official reappeared to take a second sample. After a further period of silence the farmer, losing patience, enquired the outcome of the tests, occasioning the appearance on his farm of the official for the third time, to take yet another sample. He thereafter informed the bemused farmer that it had been thought necessary to confirm the rather surprising results of the first two visits, before letting it be known that the water in his well was ninety-nine per cent pure. The sad footnote has to be added that mains water is now available and the well has been capped with concrete.

Further west but still on the north coast is Llanbadrig (GR 376947); with the help of the Ordnance Survey map the church will be found about a mile east of Cemaes Bay (*Cemais*), perched perilously on the cliff top above the sea. A more exposed and wind-swept position for a church can hardly be imagined; tradition has it that St Patrick suffered shipwreck on his way to Ireland and was cast ashore on a little island that lies about half a mile off-shore, now known as Ynys Badrig. Eventually reaching the sanctuary of the mainland, he is credited with having founded a church here as a thank-offering for his survival before proceeding to his momentous task of Christianising Ireland. All this was in the fifth century; the present church shows no sign of being older than the thirteenth or the fourteenth century. It suffered grievously in 1985, when vandals set fire to it, after stealing inflammatory material from the farm next to the church. In the blaze half the roof and much of the porch were destroyed, along with some of the pews but by dint of an almost superhuman effort of fund-raising on the part of friends of the church, the damage was made good and the church reconsecrated in 1987. The churchyard, almost alone of the churchyards to be visited, is not graced by a single yew tree, which is hardly surprising in view of its geographical position. Burials have taken place all round the church; of particular interest are five vertical seventeenth century grave slabs, all with clear inscriptions, three of which stand up in the porch, with the other two propping up the porch from the outside, dated 1652 and 1677. The only other building in the immediate neighbourhood is the farm next to the church, called Ty'n Llan, whose name, Church House, indicates that in earlier centuries it had played an important part in the life of the church, as the church-warden usually kept his account books there and other essential appurtenances.

Llan-faes (GR 605779) is about a mile north of Beaumaris, where in 1295 Edward 1st caused a castle to be built, English immigrants being thereafter induced to settle there in the new town that had been laid out to suit their needs. Llan-faes, already

Llangadwaladr

Llaneilian

a prosperous community, thanks to its fertile soil and its well-organised agricultural way of life, was thought by Edward 1st to present an intolerable threat to the wellbeing of Beaumaris. Hence in 1303 its inhabitants, by royal decree, were forcibly removed to the other side of the island, where a purpose-built town awaited them at Newborough. Today the medieval church at Llanfaes still stands, in a delightful rural situation, from which all hustle and bustle seem to have ebbed away. The churchyard is round and raised, suggesting the possibility of a Bronze Age settlement. The yew trees are large and ancient, and just outside the church porch is a medieval cross on the stumped shaft of which rests an eighteenth century sundial.

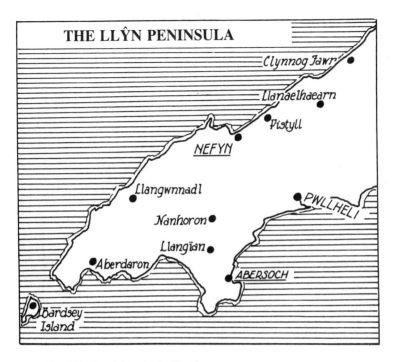

THE LLŶN PENINSULA

Clynnog fawr

Llanaelhaearn

Pistyll

NEFYN

Llangwnnadl

Nanhoron

Llangian

Aberdaron

PWLLHELI

ABERSOCH

Bardsey
Island

B. The Pilgrims' Route to Bardsey

Before detailing which churchyards are to be visited on the
Pilgrims' Route to Bardsey, it seems reasonable to put the idea of
going on pilgrimages into context. In the ancient world, long
before the advent of Christianity, periodic visits to places of
religious interest were popular, especially in India. The idea in
consequence had grown up that it was incumbent upon the
devotees of a particular religion to visit those holy places which
were associated with their religious beliefs. While not insisting
that early Christians consciously imitated this practice, it was
none the less natural that visits should be paid to places that had
loomed large in the life and ministry of Jesus Christ. Bethlehem
and Jerusalem in particular became popular venues for the first
Christian pilgrims. Although here in the west there was no
tradition of pilgrimages in pre-Christian times on which to build,
it gradually became the practice of Christians who had the means

71

and the opportunities to travel to go to Rome, in order to venerate the places where Peter and Paul had been martyred. For those who were never going to have the chance to travel such a great distance, substitute journeys were to present themselves over the years to compensate for their inability to visit Rome. One of these short range pilgrimages was to the sacred island of Bardsey (*Ynys Enlli*), situated about three miles south-west of the Llŷn Peninsula.

Early in the sixth century, probably in 516, St Cadfan, one of the first of the immensely important band of Celtic missionaries, established a monastery on Bardsey Island, which was to become a power-house for the training of missionaries who were to go forth and convert the pagan Celts of North Wales. The precise circumstances which prompted the idea of an actual pilgrimage to Bardsey are shrouded in obscurity, but it is quite certain that the momentum of pilgrimage to Bardsey received a great fillip early in the following century. The year 615 was a black year in the annals of the Celts, because at the battle of Chester in that year not only was a Celtic army heavily defeated by an Anglo-Saxon force, but the latter also saw fit to put to the sword fifteen hundred of the two thousand four hundred monks, who lived in the neighbouring monastery at Bangor Is-coed, unarmed monks, who were cut down while they were praying for their fellow Celts on the battle-field. Their monastery was destroyed and the surviving nine hundred monks fled — by stages — to Bardsey, taking advantage of the main hospices which had been organised in the churchyards en route. These refugees greatly strengthened the monastery of St Cadfan, when they settled in the island. Four of these churchyards on the way to Bardsey will now be described: Clynnog Fawr, Llanaelhaearn, Pistyll and Llangwnnadl.

Clynnog Fawr (GR 414409) is a large village on the A499, about ten miles south-west of Caernarfon; its parish church, dedicated to St Beuno, is one of the most outstanding churches in the whole of Wales. It is the St Davids of the North. Beuno, who, according to folk-lore, ministered as a young man in Berriew, today a handsome, black and white village, south-west of Welshpool, one day was so disturbed to see a Saxon walking on the further bank of the Severn, that he decamped to the west, where he had the good fortune to be given by a descendant of Cunedda a tract of land near the sea. Here at Clynnog Fawr he built a llan, the forerunner of a later clas, which was to acquire a very great reputation. All this happened early in the seventh century; the essential supply of water for this settlement was provided by a well, which still flourishes a few hundred yards down the road towards Llanaelhaearn. At this time pilgrims were already passing that way; the well, whose supply of water was always sufficient to satisfy all pilgrim needs, in time became very famous for the curative properties of its water.

When Beuno died later in the seventh century, he was buried in his chapel, which became a shrine not only for pilgrims but also for the sick. It was fondly believed that great benefit accrued to sick persons, if, after bathing in the well, they were carried to St Beuno's chapel, where they had to pass the night on his table tomb. This tradition died very hard, Pennant as late as in 1770, commenting that he had himself seen a patient late at night resting on the famous tomb. This chapel was devastated by the Vikings in 978 but was subsequently restored to act as a monastery and hospice, which catered for the needs of pilgrims well past the Middle Ages, even surviving the Dissolution of the Monasteries.

Today's magnificent church was mostly built in the fifteenth and sixteenth centuries and was connected in the seventeenth century by a stone passage to St Beuno's chapel which too was rebuilt in the sixteenth century. What was believed to have been Beuno's tomb-stone managed to survive until the nineteenth century when it disappeared, when the chapel became a school, in about 1850. Of special interest in the church is a chest, hewn out of a single log; it is inevitably known as St Beuno's Chest, though it certainly belongs to the Middle Ages. A curious tradition grew up that throws some light on the saint's posthumous reputation; all lambs and calves who at birth were observed to have a nick in their ears were said to belong to St Beuno. Farmers who had lambs and calves with this distinguishing mark were compelled by custom to bring them to church the following Trinity Sunday when the churchwarden sold them, putting the proceeds into St Beuno's chest. This medieval practice lasted well into the nineteenth century.

The large churchyard has an eighteenth century lychgate opposite the east end of the church and there are two interesting and unexplained stones, possibly glacial erratics, near the church, the largest being only an inch from the north wall. Pride of place in the churchyard must however go to the Celtic sundial, cut into the vertical southern face of a pillar stone, which stands about six feet south of the south-west corner of St Beuno's chapel. This impressive sundial is far older than any other part of the church and is probably the second oldest churchyard sundial in the countries of Britain. In 1950 the ancient pilgrimage to Bardsey was revived; the pilgrims, a large number of them, gathered in the church where they were addressed by the Bishop of Bangor before he led them out on to the road to Bardsey. More will be said about this modern pilgrimage when the little pilgrim church of Pistyll is visited.

Three miles south-west of Clynnog Fawr, on the B4417, three hundred feet above sea level, is Llanaelhaearn (GR 387448), sited against the dramatic background afforded by Yr Eifl, whose rugged outline looms a further sixteen hundred feet above the hilly village. Here in the early seventh century, St Aelhaearn set up a llan, which was to become the nucleus of the village that still bears his name; Aelhaearn, one of three brothers, all Christian missionaries, was a pupil of St Beuno, who probably trained him in his clas at Clynnog Fawr. Not far from the church, which is fittingly dedicated to Aelhaearn, is a well, marked on the O.S. map as Ffynnon Aelhaearn, whose seemingly unending flow of water has sufficed to satisfy all local needs from early times to the present. The excellence of this water supply attracted not only Aelhaearn but also the pilgrims who were to make Llanaelhaearn one of their resting places on their way to Bardsey. When in 1892 the parish church was rebuilt, a number of inscriptions were found on inside walls, which were thought to have been the graffiti of pilgrims in the Middle Ages. Also in the church, on the west wall will be seen a memorial stone, belonging to the sixth century, which was brought into the church from a field, next to the churchyard, known as the Garden of the Saints.

Clynnog Fawr

Pistyll

It commemorates one Aliortus, who the quite legible inscription informs us came from Elmet, a very far distant Celtic outpost, east of the Pennines. Another sixth century memorial stone still stands in probably its original position in the churchyard, between the gate and the west door of the church. It is interesting to speculate that it is quite possible that the funeral of the man named on the stone, Melitus, was conducted by Aelhaearn himself. Also in the churchyard are some large, and therefore ancient yew trees and a number of table tombs, whose stone walls carry horizontal slabs, made of slate.

Continue on the B4417 for about four miles in a south-westerly direction towards Nefyn but just before the village of Pistyll is reached turn right on to a very minor road, which very soon after passing a hotel peters out at a farm and the church. The farm is straight on but the church is on a raised mound on the right; Pistyll church (GR 328423) is dedicated to St Beuno, whose well is near at hand. Pistyll was a very important staging post on the pilgrim route to Bardsey; where the farm now stands, there was in much earlier times a monastery, whose inmates made themselves responsible for the welfare of the pilgrims. The fish-pond, which served the monks and, it is to be hoped, the pilgrims too, stands by the side of the road below the church, which was built on the site of the original wattle and daub huts of the first llan there. On the very steep slopes of the mound on which the church was built are to be seen all manner of berry-bearing bushes, hawthorns, hops, sloes, blackberries and gooseberries, all of which may well have been planted thereabouts by the monks, who supplied food and drink to the pilgrims. In addition, in the churchyard itself may still be found medicinal herbs, which were probably first planted there in the Middle Ages.

Possibly as a direct result of the idea of a pilgrimage being revived in Clynnog in 1950, here at Pistyll devoted friends of the church have, three times a year now for forty years, at Christmas, Easter and at Lammas, strewn the church floor with rushes and decorated the entire church with medicinal herbs and other plants gathered from the churchyard and the mound, thus bringing the past back much nearer to the present. In Pistyll

Aberdaron

today the visitor with a seeing eye can very easily acquire a sense of another age, when less attention was devoted to the satisfaction of creature comforts and the gratification of material goals.

Llangwnnadl (GR 208333), last of the pilgrim resting places to be visited, is situated about five miles short of Aberdaron; two miles south of Tudweiliog leave the B4417, taking a righthand turning on to a minor road that leads to the church, which is dedicated to St Gwynhoedl. He was a sixth century missionary who was the first to make use of this site, building his wattle and daub hut here, when he set up a llan. From the earliest times pilgrims chose this spot as their last resting place, where they could prepare themselves for the ordeal that lay ahead of them, of crossing over to Bardsey. The pilgrims rested and relaxed in the field next to the churchyard; as the pilgrimage grew ever more popular, so the church had to be extended to cater for their needs, this explaining the need for a triple-naved church.

The claim of the Ashmolean Museum in Oxford to have the care of St Gwynhoedl's tombstone was challenged in 1940, when in a plaster-stripping exercise on the interior south wall there was revealed a slab that bore a cross carved in a ring, which still bore traces of the original red paint. Further evidence of the saint's burial has been inferred from an inscription on a pillar on the north arcade, which reads S. GWYNHOEDL IACET HIC.

The churchyard today contains many good examples of table tombs, from the seventeenth to the end of the nineteenth centuries, while south of the church is the base of a medieval churchyard cross, which is surmounted by a shaft that was stumped in the seventeenth century, only to be brought back into use in the eighteenth century when a horizontal sundial was set upon its top.

In Aberdaron (GR 173264) the church stands on the very edge of the beach, the churchyard wall shored up against the storms. In early days, before the church was built, the pilgrims probably waited for their boat inland. In modern Aberdaron, which tends in the season to lose something of its charm and character by the very pressure of population, there is a white house in the middle of the village, Y Gegin Fawr (*the Big Kitchen*), where holiday-makers today buy food and drink just as the pilgrims did in the Middle Ages in the same old building.

Of Bardsey itself little need here be said, beyond stating that something like twenty thousand Christians are buried there and that the church authorities in Rome were so impressed by Bardsey that they decreed that three pilgrimages to the island would be reckoned as the equal of one pilgrimage to Rome itself. Perhaps the last comment may be left to Giraldus Cambrensis who, visiting Bardsey in 1188, wrote: "Either because of its pure air or through some miracle occasioned by the merits of the holy men who live there, the island has the peculiarity that no-one dies there except in extreme old age, for disease is almost unheard of. . ." Indeed the isle of the blest!

Bardsey (Aerial)

79

C. Here and There in Gwynedd

In the last two chapters two parts of Gwynedd have already been treated, Anglesey and the Llŷn Peninsula, but Gwynedd covers so wide and diverse an area, embracing as it does the former counties of Caernarfon and Meirionnydd, that three more districts will be visited, the Dee Valley, the Conwy Valley and the district around Dolgellau. Corwen (GR 079434) lies about ten miles west of Llangollen on the A5 near the spot where the river Alwen joins the Dee. Before men settled at this confluence, however, they had lived up above on a neighbouring hill, a mile to the north. This place, Caer Drewyn (GR 087444) seems to have served the needs of its inhabitants for very many years, as there are archaeological indications of successive cultures there. It was certainly being lived in during the Iron Age, when the Roman legions passed down below and probably survived the departure of the Romans more than three hundred years later.

South-west of Corwen in the upper part of the Dee Valley on the way to Bala there is considerable evidence of much earlier activity — still in the Bronze Age. Indeed it is quite likely that men and women of the Bronze Age actually settled for a while in Corwen itself but the evidence for this is not conclusive, depending as it does on the fact that today's churchyard is round and raised and that there is in the churchyard a stone which could well have belonged to a Bronze Age alignment. (A brief reference to this was made in the second chapter of the first part of this book.)

Both in Wales and also in other parts of Britain folk memory insists that in the early days of building churches the devout Christians, thus engaged, were sometimes thwarted by supernatural forces from building on sites which they had selected. Here in Corwen there is a strong local tradition that several attempts at laying foundations came to nought through the intervention of these same supernatural forces. Finally the holy men were allowed to build on a site, which, it seems, was already hallowed in local memory by the presence nearby of a large and ancient stone. In later years, when the need arose to

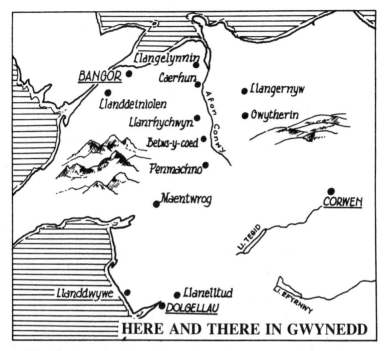

HERE AND THERE IN GWYNEDD

add a porch to the church, it was found necessary to incorporate the stone into the east wall of the porch, as the original church had been built as near as possible to the all-important stone. In more recent times the inside wall of the porch has been plastered over, but from the outside this possible in situ remainder of the Bronze Age is still clearly visible.

Another feature of the churchyard is the survival on the south side, quite close to the wall of the church, of a Celtic cross, belonging to the ninth century. Though it may not be thought relevant in the context of Corwen's churchyard to refer to Owain Glyndŵr, it is difficult not to mention him, because as a favoured local son (he had an estate in the Dee Valley a few miles to the east of Corwen) he is frequently thought to have intervened in local affairs. A mark on this Celtic cross is believed by some to have been caused by the angry despatch of a dagger by the great man, while what seems likely to be a consecration cross on the door of the Priest's entrance on the south side of the church is also attributed to a spear thrown in pique by Owain Glyndŵr from a nearby hill! In fact there was another Owain, who figured more prominently in local affairs, Owain Gwynedd, who, nearly two hundred years earlier in the twelfth century gathered an army on Caer Drewyn to oppose the expected invasion of the Dee Valley by Henry II, an attack which in the event was diverted by the timely intervention of a very wet August!

Returning to the churchyard, which is a very large one, it will be noticed that many good eighteenth century horizontal gravestones have been taken up and rearranged to form a necessary series of steps in the hillier part of the churchyard, while immediately behind the church on the south side some eighteenth century buildings have encroached upon the churchyard. These are almshouses, known as the College, which were put up by a Shropshire man, William Eyton, to provide accommodation for the widows of clergymen.

Three churchyards have been chosen in the Conwy Valley, all for various reasons rarely visited today; one at the southern end of the valley is around the old church at Betws-y-coed, the second is at Llanrhychwyn in the hills above Trefriw, while the third is further north and much higher in the hills at Llangelynnin, which was referred to in Chapter 4 of Part 1 in connection with its well-preserved well.

Llangelynnin (GR 752737) is difficult to find but is worth a long and probably arduous search; once there the visitor can get some insight into life in these parts in the Middle Ages, when this tract of high land was more lived in than it is now. It is perhaps hard to grasp, when standing on the bleak hill behind the churchyard, that St Celynnin's church and churchyard once played an important part in the social life of this remote parish, constituting an oasis in this wild upland area, where religious and social needs were equally catered for. Certainly games were played in the unconsecrated north side of the churchyard — indeed at one time there was even a cockpit there.

On the south side many table tombs have survived but undoubtedly the most significant activities that went on, outside in the churchyard, were centred on the well, whose reputation for curing the diseases, especially of children, was more than

Corwen — 9th c. cross

Llangelynnin, Conwy Valley

local. Sick children were brought from a distance and were housed in local farms, while they underwent treatment at St Celynnin's well.

Moving south along the B5106 Llanrhychwyn (GR 775616) may be approached either from Trefriw or up a finger-posted minor road opposite Llanrwst; both roads are steep and narrow — a local enquiry may save a lot of time. Llywelyn ab Iorwerth, who earned the title of "the Great", built a court at Trefriw, after marrying King John's illegitimate daughter, Joan. Llywelyn and his wife thereafter followed the steep path to worship at Llanrhychwyn, which in after years came in consequence to be called "the old church of Llywelyn".

Forty years ago, when first visited by the author, something of its past glory still lingered on in the double-naved church, set in a meadow, with its steep roof and low door almost hidden by the protection afforded by the great yew trees. The church still stands, of course, so do the yews but sheep now graze among the graves and the door of the church is open to the weather. Inside the church much is as it was, with the hand bier still hanging on the west wall. The lintel over the lych-gate still bears the initials of the churchwardens who put it up in 1762. However, it is hard to remember that the churchyard once presented an animated scene, when the air re-echoed with the cries of pleasure as ball games were being played against the sturdy walls of the church, although on the south side of the west front a few scoring marks may still with difficulty be made out. The farm next to the church, interestingly named Ty'n Llan, *Church House*, recalls happier times when the churchwardens regulated all activities in the churchyard and had the oversight of the social life of the parish.

Back down the tortuous lane to the B5106 and the road to Betws-y-coed, where the churchyard that surrounds the old church near the railway station (GR 795565) is a peaceful place indeed, that recalls the more spacious times when this church served the local community. It is splendidly situated near the river and the churchyard is carefully and lovingly maintained. Gone, of course, are the days when this churchyard acted as the village playground, though signs of the popularity of ball games

Llanrhychwyn — lych gate

St Michael's, Betws-y-coed, old church

85

are still visible on the outside walls of the nave. The yew trees, though ancient and immense, are healthy and the eighteenth century is well represented by the lych-gate, the sundial and a number of table tombs.

The last churchyard to be visited in Gwynedd is two miles north west of Dolgellau at Llanelltud (GR 717195); the name invites a comment, as the church is the only one to be dedicated to St Illtud in North Wales, although his brother Sadwrn lived, ministered artd died even further north in Anglesey. The circumstances which brought the great missionary, who probably hailed from Brittany, to the Mawddach estuary are unknown, but in addition to the great seminary which he founded at Llanilltud Fawr in Glamorgan (Llantwit Major), he is known to have lived in the Gower peninsula (at Oystermouth and Oxwich), and in Powys at Llanhamlach (with a neolithic long barrow named after him near Brecon Tŷ Illtud!). Also in the Brecon Breacons a hill bears his honoured name, Mynydd Illtud, as does a Bronze Age round barrow, Bedd Illtud, while some will insist that he was buried nearby in a churchyard not far from the Mountain Centre at Libanus. Sometime in the first half of the sixth century Illtud sought out a small hill above the Mawddach and there established a llan, before presumably returning to the Brecon Beacons. In time more permanent buildings were put up on the same site and it is known that at the end of the thirteenth century there was a substantial stone church there. Not far from the church the Cistercians in 1199 founded a monastery at Cymer Abbey, and from then until its dissolution in the middle of the sixteenth century the monks from the abbey supplied the church of Llanelltud with priests.

The church today is well-attended and in consequence the churchyard is well-maintained; it is in an incomparable position, enjoying panoramic views of Cader Idris to the south. The churchyard is round and raised, and approached through an avenue of yews. Elsewhere in the churchyard there are other large yews, a number of eighteenth century horizontal graves and at the west end of the churchyard a remarkable late nineteenth century table tomb, with a deeply carved palm frond standing proud of the lid.

On the north side in front of all the windows gudgeons remain on which hinged shutters once hung; there is further evidence of shuttering in former days on the windows on the west wall too. In both cases protection against damage was being sought from the ball games which were played against the walls here, as in so many other Welsh churchyards. Also, not far away, is an old house, long since restored, which was sometimes called Yr Hen Dafarn (*the old inn*), at other times Ty'n Llan (*the church house*). Here in former times worshippers were able after service to slake their thirsts with a less heady brew than was obtainable elsewhere in the neighbourhood. The steps in the churchyard wall are thought to have been originally cut to provide an easy route from church to inn! Inside the church, at the west end of the nave, stands a curious stone, which bears the imprint of a foot, associated with a pilgrim, who is believed to have made his mark in this way, before setting out on a twelfth century pilgrimage, possibly to Bardsey. It was found under a pile of rubbish in a hut near the church and brought inside in 1876.

The author learnt too late to make the necessary change in the text that he had in error placed Corwen in Gwynedd. For his mistake, he apologises to all concerned.

D. The Northern Marches

Llanynys (GR 103627), situated in the Vale of Clwyd betwen Denbigh and Ruthin, is rather a special place. It was given its name, suggesting an island llan, because the earliest building was put on a low mound above the swampy land that lay between the rivers Clwyd and Clywedog. In the winter months it must frequently have stood out like an island above the flooded valley.

By the sixth century the monastic movement was developing fast in Wales. In the previous century Celtic missionaries had tended to live their simple, devoted lives in isolation, in their primitive huts in their llans, but gradually their work had become more centralised as they were organised to live together with other priests in clasau, monasteries, which thereafter frequently also became important centres of learning and culture. Llanilltud and Llancarfan spring to mind as early examples of excellence in this field. Here in Llanynys in the sixth century such a clas was established, a monastic community, presided over by an abbot. Nothing, of course, of this clas has survived but on this same site another church grew and prospered, making it possible today for the thoughtful observer to recreate in the mind's eye this early place of learning and devotion, while at the same time enjoying the treasures that the intervening years have stored up in this church and churchyard.

Llanynys is hard to find but not easy to forget, although today it only amounts to an inn, a private house and the church, in front of whose main gate stands on the lefthand side a mounting block while set into the wall on the right is a Victorian post-box. It seems desirable in Llanynys to treat church and churchyard as one entity, especially as one of the most interesting and historically valuable objects in the church stood in the churchyard until thirty years ago. It is a carved sepulchral stone, now to be seen in the west end of the church, which dates from the fourteenth century and is believed to have had associations with St Saeran, to whom the present church is dedicated.

Behind it on the north wall, the traditional place where all might be expected to look, is a fifteenth century wall painting of St Christopher, the patron saint of travellers, whose help may

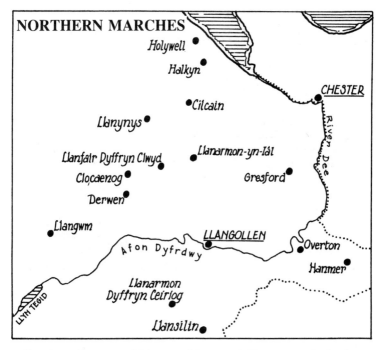

NORTHERN MARCHES

Holywell
Halkyn
Cilcain
Llanynys
Llanarmon-yn-Iâl
Llanfair Dyffryn Clwyd
Clocaenog
Gresford
Derwen
Llangwm
CHESTER
River Dee
LLANGOLLEN
Afon Dyfrdwy
Overton
Hanmer
Llanarmon
Dyffryn Ceiriog
Llansilin
LLYN TEGID

often have been sought by worshippers at Llanynys, who had on foot or on horseback to find their way back home to dry land. Fortunately this quite wonderful mural was not discovered until 1967 with the result that it received the most sensitive and expert treatment.

The stout south door on which in the sixteenth century several parishoners saw fit to carve both their names and the date, is further embellished with a rare sanctuary ring, while those who like to see in churches some evidence of the social history of other days, will relish the sight of a pair of dog tongs! Outside, the peaceful churchyard is round and unsurprisingly graced by a number of ancient yew trees; there are too some well-preserved table tombs. All in all, Llanynys is an ancient Welsh treasure house, which to the discerning has an exciting tale to unfold.

Cilcain (GR 177652), like Llanynys, was formerly in Flintshire; it is hidden in an intricate maze of up-country narrow roads to the west of Mold on the north-east flanks of Moel Fama.

Llansilin, Clwyd — sun-dial on shaft

Llanarmon-yn-Iâl, Clwyd — shaft of medieval cross

90

The village has a goodly number of attractive old houses and the whole area is rich in prehistoric remains, having known much activity in the Bronze Age, especially on Moel Arthur, which lies to the west of the village. Entrance to the churchyard is through an old lych-gate to which was built on in 1810 a hearse house. The churchyard is oval, the shape having been decided upon, according to one local authority, in order to furnish "no place where the demons could lurk"! A similar sentiment will be referred to later in this book, when Penbryn is visited in Dyfed! In the church, which is dedicated to St Mary and, like so many in these parts, very drastically restored in the nineteenth century, much of great value remains from earlier times, more particularly some sixteenth century stained glass and a splendid hammerbeam roof over the nave. South of the church door there stood in the Middle Ages a churchyard cross, whose truncated shaft still bears witness to its former glory.

About three miles south of the bustling town of Ruthin on the A525 road to Wrexham is Llanfair Dyffryn Clwyd (GR 135555); the church is double-naved and doubly dedicated, to St Cynfarch and St Mary. Large and old and severely restored in the late nineteenth century, the church stands in a churchyard, which is note-worthy for its yew trees and a sundial, which in 1800 was set upon the top of the broken shaft of a medieval preaching cross on the south side, close to the church door. There is a good lych-gate, dated 1708, while an interesting feature opposite the south door of the church is a large vestry house, built in 1831. Together the church and churchyard provide a peaceful oasis, as the cars rush by on the main road outside.

Five miles east of Llanfair Dyffryn Clwyd, as the crow flies but not as the road finds its way round the Clwyd Hills, is the village of Llanarmon-yn-Iâl (GR 189562); this is a nuclear settlement, clustered around the church, which is dedicated to St Garmon, to whom there are several other similar dedications in North Wales. Certainly there was a llan set up here in the sixth century on this site, on which a succession of churches has since been built, the present one having been begun late in the thirteenth century and much enlarged two centuries later. The churchyard is round and has an interesting hearse house; on the south-east

91

side stands the broken shaft of a medieval cross, to which was added a sundial in 1772, an addition which found no favour with the writer of the church notes, who complains "the mason being paid three shillings for this act of vandalism". The sundial no longer adorns the shaft. The area just south of the village contains limestone caves, where much neolithic evidence has been found; in 1896 a pair of well-made prehistoric axes were discovered there, which have since been traced to the well-known Craig Lwyd stone axe factory near Penmaenmawr.

South-east of Chirk the beautiful Ceiriog Valley runs up into the Berwyn hills; at the top of the valley is Llanarmon Dyffryn Ceiriog (GR 158328), whose church, like the last one visited, is dedicated to St Garmon. It is sited on rising ground at the far end of the village. The churchyard is round and possesses a number of yew trees, two enormous specimens of which, close to each other, just west of the west door of the church suggest the original approach. Between these yews and the entrance to the churchyard there is a man-made mound, which has a stone set on top of it, which in former times bore a sundial. No one seems to know why this mound was made; at Llanfechain, further south in Powys, which will be described in the next chapter, there is a similar mound in the churchyard, the origin of which is likewise unknown. To add to the mystery this church at Llanfechain is also dedicated to St Garmon.

No account of Llanarmon is adequate that makes no reference to the two picturesque hotels that face each other in the middle of the village. George Borrow passed that way a century and a half ago; he entered one of the hostelries, called for ale, and, as was his custom, engaged his neighbour in conversation. He was a local waggoner and he had a newspaper spread out in front of him. Borrow enquired about the news, only to be told that the waggoner was unable to read. George Borrow, never one to walk away from a delicate situation, then countered with "Why then are you looking at the paper?" Back came the surprising reply "Because by looking at the letters I hope in time to make them out."

This chapter, which began with a visit to a clas church at Llanynys, finishes with a visit to another clas church at Llansilin

Llanfair Dyffryn Clwyd, Clwyd — vestry house

(GR 209281), which is a most attractive village of considerable size; it is less than ten miles from Oswestry, but it is a very long way from any main road and seemingly unaffected by the less pleasant distractions of modern life. Streams and wooded hills abound in this fortunate place. The present church, built on the site of the former clas, dedicated to St Silin, was erected in the fourteenth century and thoroughly and sensitively restored about a hundred years ago. It contains many excellent features, which are outside the scope of this chapter.

The large and well-tended churchyard has a number of gnarled yews, three of which are particularly outstanding The inscriptions on the many table tombs provide social historians with much useful information. South of the porch there is, as in so many Welsh churchyards, the broken shaft of a medieval preaching cross, brought back into use in later days by the addition of a horizontal bronze sundial.

The seventeenth century Welsh lyric poet, Huw Morus (1622-1709), who was born in the Ceiriog Valley, died in Llansilin, where his grave may still be seen in the churchyard, close to the south wall of the chancel. George Borrow, after drinking up his ale with the waggoner in Llanarmon, walked over the hills to Llansilin, where he persuaded the publican of the next inn he patronised to take him to the churchyard and show him the grave of Huw Morus. This the publican did and "forthwith", George Borrow wrote "taking off my hat, I went down on my knees and kissed the cold slab covering the cold remains of the mighty Huw."

2. POWYS

A. The Central Marches

When in 1974 the name Powys was resurrected from the limbo of the past to become one of the new administrative divisions of Wales, the three disparate counties of Montgomeryshire, Radnorshire and Brecknockshire, which had been created by the Act of Union in 1536, lost their separate identities. This section of the book, The Central Marches, concerns itself only with Montgomeryshire, which is now the largest and most populous of the three constituent parts.

In these border lands between the lowlands and the high hills a great many men of differing types and temperaments have passed through, nomads and settlers, men of war and men of peace. It is a land of castles and fortified places and of Offa's

95

Dyke, but all that was yesterday. Today it constitutes an oasis, free at last from the passage of strangers and their warring factions.

Five churchyards have with difficulty been singled out for individual attention, with difficulty because there are few churchyards hereabouts that have no special contribution to make, be it, as at Tregynon (GR 097987) where there is a large sundial on the church tower where a clock would be expected, or at Montgomery (*Trefaldwyn*, GR 224965) with its avenue of yews above the sunken churchyard approach to the church door, or at Aberhafesb, west of Newtown (*Y Drenewydd*, GR 073924) where the churchyard is adorned by a vast yew tree many centuries old.

Four miles east of the market town of Llanfyllin is the village of Llanfechain (GR 189204), which has the good fortune to be by-passed from the main road, the B4393; the village, grouped around its Norman parish church, stands, like Llanfyllin, on the River Cain, as the name Llanfechain implies. A mile or two further east the Cain becomes swallowed up in the river Fyrnwy (*Vyrnwy*), itself a tributary of the Severn. The church is on a raised and circular site, which could well have been used by earlier people in the Bronze Age. The evidence for such a theory is the raised nature of the site, the fact that it is circular, the presence north of today's church of a mound, which may have been a round barrow in the Bronze Age, and the existence of a plentiful supply of water not too far away. At any rate in the sixth century a Christian missionary, St Garmon, whose name is associated too with five other churches in North Wales, is believed to have built the first church at Llanfechain, sanctifying the area and giving his name to the mound north of the church, still known as Garmon's Mound, on whose gentle slopes may be seen many nineteenth and twentieth century grave-stones. He likewise is thought to have blessed the well, St Garmon's Well, which is about three hundred yards away, in consequence of which water for centuries thereafter was drawn to supply the font of the church. Tradition has it too that St Garmon caused a yew tree to be planted near the well: be that as it may, this tree that bore his name was destroyed by fire about eighty years ago, from surviving timbers of which a lectern was fashioned which is still in use in the church.

The southern approach to the church today is marked by an avenue of rhododendrons, a not uncommon sight in the churchyards of Montgomeryshire; also south of the church is a sundial, which surmounts a purpose-built nineteenth century shaft, similar to others in the neighbourhood, though its base is probably that of the medieval churchyard cross. South and east of the church around the periphery of the churchyard are some sturdy yew trees, while north of the church in that part of the churchyard that was unconsecrated in the Middle Ages there is evidence of a former cock pit.

A few miles south of Llanfechain and about two and a half miles north of Welshpool is the far from remote village of Guilsfield (GR 219117), its Welsh name is Cegidfa. In the Middle Ages the village grew up around the church but in the second half of the twentieth century much building development has taken place at the opposite end of the village which has had the effect of leaving the church and churchyard well away from the busy modern settlement. The first church at Guilsfield was built towards the end of the sixth century and was dedicated to St Aelhaearn, one of three brothers, all Christian missionaries, who hailed from Caereinion, west of Welshpool. In later days this same Aelhaearn, as has already been told, became a pupil of the great St Beuno, at Clynnog Fawr, at a time when the church at Llanaelhaearn in the Llŷn Peninsula was being dedicated to him. As Beuno himself migrated to Clynnog from Berriew, south of Welshpool, it is highly likely that Aelhaearn knew him, when the church was being put up here in Guilsfield.

The very extensive round churchyard, where burying no longer takes place, is islanded by a circular road along which stand many old and interesting stone houses, both large and small. Within the churchyard wall is a ring of large yew trees, which provide a fitting frame for the visual excellence of the church whose tower offers admonitory advice to the passer-by "BE DILIGENT, NIGHT COMETH." The churchyard treasures many immense yews and many eighteenth and nineteenth century tombstones, some of the epitaphs of which merit attention. Quite near the entrance to the churchyard is one such grave, which bears a skull and cross-bones; it marks the burial of an old parishoner of ninety, who died in 1707. The accompanying epitaph informs us that the yew tree that bends over his grave was planted there by himself, when a boy in the company of his father. Nearer to the church is a nineteenth century memorial stone to a farmer's wife, who was only 36 years old when she died in 1849; her epitaph contains a solemn warning:

> Our life hangs by a single thread
> Which soon is cut and we are dead
> Then boast not, reader, of thy might,
> Alive at noon and dead at night.

In some old churches the porch was so much concerned with the secular life of the parish that what went on there frequently came to be regarded as the continuation of what went on in the churchyard, which itself was the very hub of parish life. In the two-storeyed porch at Guilsfield, there is on the ground floor an ancient oaken chest, seven feet six inches long, carved from one log, and up above an all-purpose room, which in later years became the village schoolroom, while built on to the west side of the porch is a hearse house, on which are carved the names of the churchwardens who were responsible for its erection in 1739.

Three and a half miles west of Guilsfield is the very large village of Meifod (GR 155132). It is pleasantly situated in a wooded valley through which flows the river Fyrnwy. If the size of the village surprises the visitor, then he will be positively amazed by the size of the church and even more so by the immensity of the churchyard, which in all comprises no fewer than nine acres. A leisurely walk inside the churchyard but around the perimeter is recommended in order to get some feel of the place and some sense of its significance. The churchyard really is a considerable park with numerous groups of various types of trees under which many graves are scattered.

Today's church, the third, has a twin dedication, to St Tysilio and St Mary; the first church on the site, made presumably of

Llanfechain — sun-dial

Guilsfield — 1707 tombstone of a 90 year old
who, as a boy, helped his father to plant the yew tree behind his grave

wood and wattle and daub, was put up in the middle of the sixth century by a missionary St Gwyddfarch, who probably came from Brittany. (According to local tradition, his grave is to be found on a hill-top a mile to the south-west of the village, marked Gwely Gwyddfarch.) This flimsy structure in the original llan was succeeded in the late seventh or early eighth century by another and more substantial church, built rather to the east of the earlier one by St Tysilio, who, as well as being a Christian missionary, was also, a son of the Prince of Powys. This church, which was dedicated to him, in the course of time became a clas, with great authority over a wide area, including Guilsfield; its churchyard also became so important that it is believed to have become the burial ground for the princes of Powys. The third church was begun in the twelfth century, under the auspices of another Prince of Powys; it was dedicated to St Mary and it is basically the church of today, with, of course, many additions made in later centuries. It is a quite magnificent triple-naved church, whose many features of interest have no relevance in this chapter. The oldest gravestone in the churchyard stands up against the south wall and commemorates a burial in 1670, while also on the south side of the churchyard there is a nineteenth century sundial, very similar to the one already described in the churchyard at Llanfechain.

Moving south through Welshpool on to the A483, turn right after five miles on to the B4385, and follow the signpost to Berriew (GR 188008). In Welsh, Berriew is known as Aberriw, marking the confluence of the rivers Rhiw and Severn. Here many centuries ago men lived and fought. Not only was the junction of the rivers important but also the nearby ford — a great deal of human history can be attributed to man's dislike of getting his feet wet! Berriew today is popular with visitors; its wealth of black and white houses on both sides of the river Rhiw make it perhaps even too popular in the summer months. In the middle of the village stands the church in an extensive and well-kept churchyard.

Reference has already been made in this book to St Beuno's association with Berriew, until he took fright at the nearness of the hated Saxons on the far bank of the Severn. However he must

Berriew — war memorial

have made a very considerable impact locally before he left as a Bronze Age standing stone, which stands in a field above the Severn a mile to the east of the village, is known as Maen Beuno, it being fondly believed by those who named it thus that the saint had used the stone as his pulpit! The middle of the thirteenth century proved a testing time for the people of Berriew; in 1257 Llywelyn ap Gruffudd stood firm at the ford against the forces of Henry III and gained the day; ten years later at the same spot the two men met again, this time signing a truce, whereby the King of England recognised Llywelyn ap Gruffudd as Prince of Wales, who thus became the first — and only — native Prince of Wales.

This stormy passage in Berriew's long history seems far removed from the picturesque scenes of the late twentieth century, though even now the church and churchyard sometimes provide a welcome respite when too many cars and coaches threaten the calm. The church itself, dedicated, of course, to St Beuno, belongs to modern times, having been rebuilt at the beginning of the nineteenth century and later in the same century restored by Victorian hands; the surrounding church yard is large and round with many good specimens of yew trees marking its periphery, while the approach to the church is adorned by a splendid avenue of beeches. There are a great many interesting gravestones, especially table tombs, whose inscriptions reward careful study. Proof of the respect felt locally for their patron saint is clear to those who turn aside to look at the twentieth century war memorial in the north side of the churchyard. It bears an excellent carving of St Beuno.

By way of footnote to this section on the Central Marches enthusiasts may care to make a short excursion to the hilly country east of Newtown, where the grassy uplands nourish the famous Kerry sheep. Three miles east of Newtown is the village of Kerry (*Ceri*, GR 148901) where an early settlement crystallised when the successors to the Bronze Age people who had lived in the surrounding hills decided to live more sheltered lives down below. Here in Kerry in 1176 there took place one of the most bizarre episodes ever to be recorded on consecrated ground. In that year the rebuilt church, dedicated to St Michael, was due to be reconsecrated, a duty claimed by both the sees of St Davids and St Asaph to be within their jurisdiction. The representative of St Davids, none other than the formidable Giraldus Cambrensis, hearing that his rival was already on his way, made haste to get there first. Giraldus won that race, hastened through the churchyard and burst into the church, where he ordered the bells to be rung to notify the approaching bishop that he was too late. The bishop, nothing daunted, pressed on and entered the holy precincts, where each cleric proceeded to excommunicate the other. Giraldus, however, gained the verdict as the tolling of the bells was interpreted by the people of Kerry to mean that they were to be ruled by St Davids; the poor Bishop of St Asaph received short shrift from the populace as he hurried away in defeat. Nearly seven hundred years later, however, the verdict of history was reversed, when in 1849 St Asaph was allowed to take over responsibility for the welfare of Kerry. Today all is peaceful in the round churchyard, where the yews stand sentinel; the vast tower of the church still looks as stout a fortress as it did in the Middle Ages when the men of Kerry sharpened their arrows on its lower walls as they left morning service on their way to the butts.

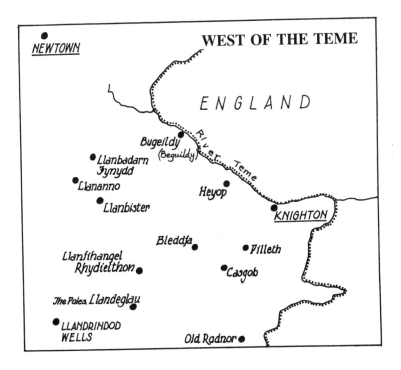

B. West of the Teme

South of Newtown the valleys of the rivers Ithon (*Ieithon*) and Teme (*Tefeidiad*) enclose wild and largely untrodden hilly country, which rises south-west of Beguildy (*Bugeildy*) to its highest point on Beacon Hill, on whose upper flanks are several tumuli. To view the churchyards west of the Teme an excursion is proposed in an anti-clockwise direction, starting and finishing at Knighton, whose Welsh name is Tref-y-clawdd, describing it as the Town on the Dyke (Offa's).

Early men who settled at all in these parts must have found the terrain forbidding, for, apart from the tumuli on Beacon Hill, evidence of their settlement is confined to a few Bronze Age round barrows in the upper Teme valley and a valuable hoard of late Bronze Age gold neck rings, dug up near Heyop, (*Llanddewi-yn-Heiob*) just north of Knighton. An Ordnance

Survey map is desirable on this excursion, which will proceed up the Teme valley from Knighton, in a north-westerly direction past Beguildy, then turn left to climb westwards over the hills before descending to the valley of the Ithon. After exploring churchyards southwards down the valley, the return to Knighton will be made over the north and eastern flanks of Radnor Forest.

Enter the Teme valley on the B4355 but after two miles, at Knucklas (*Cnwclas*), turn left for a brief diversion to Heyop (GR 240746) where the road almost ends; here the church, which will be seen on the right-hand side, was completely rebuilt in 1880 but evidence of much earlier times is provided by a yew tree of quite massive proportions, which stands by the entrance gate. On the short return journey note should be taken of a hill to the north of the road, which is a spectacular site for a castle, which indeed once dominated the landscape from Norman times until the nineteenth century, when the people of the neighbourhood took advantage of a plentiful supply of building material! The castle still exists in the local imagination, as many still fondly believe that Guinevere married King Arthur on Knucklas Hill!

Five miles further up the Teme valley on the B4355 is the village of Beguildy (GR 195798), which in the past owed its importance to the many thousands of sheep which grazed on the surrounding hills. Indeed Beguildy means "The Shepherd's House" and masses of sheep still graze there above the quiet and beautiful valley of the Teme. The church, as so often in the Marches, is built on a hill above the village; its dedication to St Michael might be owing to the proximity of Beguildy to the Radnor Forest, where a great dragon was thought to live, or more probably because of the siting of the church on raised ground where St Michael, in view of his reputation for dealing firmly with the devil, could be expected to be in a strong position for putting down his adversaries! As well as being high up, the churchyard is also round, and in consequence once again the chances have to be considered of there having been a Bronze Age settlement on the site. It also covers a considerable area, not all of which has been used for burials. There are however a great many gravestones, some of which are of outstanding quality both for their shape and for their decoration. The high standard of the stonemason's art at Beguildy, which is repeated in other churchyards in north Radnorshire, suggests the existence of a sturdy local tradition of craftmanship. Many of the best specimens date from the middle of the nineteenth century, although there are also some eighteenth century table tombs. There are a few sturdy yew trees, but the main avenue from the gate to the church door is of rhododendrons, as was also observed at Llanfechain. The church is large for a village and among other features is a very fine fifteenth century screen, which still shows some of the original colouring. An irrelevant but not uninteresting footnote comes from the local record; it seems that in 1858 the publican here was hauled before the magistrates and fined £5 (a not inconsiderable sum in those days) for drawing a pint of beer during the hours of divine service!

Continue for a further five miles along the B4355 through Felindre until a left-hand turning is reached, labelled Llanbadarn Fynydd. The GR is 120827, the mountain road quite passable, being wide enough for two cars and the surface reasonable. The panoramic view from the top is spectacular, unveiling a landscape of undulating hills with few signs of human habitation. At the bottom of the hill is Llanbadarn Fynydd (GR 098778) on the main road, A483, which runs from Newtown to Llandrindod Wells. The church is at the south end of the village, on the west side of the road; the high churchyard wall and the steeply sloping ground beyond all but hide the church, which is built on the edge of an even steeper bank above the river Ithon. The church, sited thus precariously, has no north side to its churchyard. In the porch a hand-bier is firmly secured to the rafters. The south side of the churchyard has many gravestones, some of which indicate the same high standard of craftmanship, noticed at Beguildy. There are also some eighteenth century graves — one wide, well-carved gravestone commemorates the death of a thirteen-year old boy in 1850:

> "Young men remember, die you must
> And all your glory turn to dust
> The Lord of me hath made his choice
> So, dear parents, do rejoice

'Twas He alone who knew for why
That in my youth I was to die."

Two hundred years ago there was in this part of Wales a
tradition of pugilism; the district champion, a Newtown man,
had successfully resisted a number of attempts to wrest his crown
from him until a fighter emerged from Llanbadarn Fynydd, who
dared to enter the lists. Where the fight took place is obscure but
what is known is that to the amazement of the large crowd the
invincible champion from Newtown was soundly beaten. It was
then that the Vicar of Beguildy was spotted not far away "sitting
in a yew tree with a huge book opened in front of him, directing
the evil spirits, to assist the Llanbadarn man" — clearly the
account was written by a Newtown man!

Shortly before savouring the delights of Llanbister, which lies
three miles south of Llanbadarn Fynydd, a brief stop is
recommended at the road-side, where the little church of
Llananno (GR 097744) is sited between the road and the river
Ithon. The surrounding churchyard is sombre and overgrown
but inside the church is a surprise indeed. In the second half of
the nineteenth century when church restorers were at their
busiest in Wales, it was the custom all too often to take out old
screens and make a bonfire of them in the churchyard. Here at
Llananno in 1876 the restorers did rebuild the church and they
did take out the screen but, marvellous to relate, they not only
took it back when the rebuilding was finished but also made
arrangements for it to be restored, a process which was finally
completed in 1960. Llananno's sixteenth century screen is
assuredly one of the great treasures of Wales.

Happy is the village that has not been built on a main road;
happier still is a place like Llanbister that is near enough to a
main road to be able to take advantage of its amenities without
suffering from the drawbacks of noise and pollution. A mile
south of Llananno is Llanbister (GR 111734), just around the
corner from the A483 on the B4356. On climbing up from the
village on to the slope on which the church is built, one is at once
impressed by its geographical situation near the top of a very
considerable hill; the church commands extensive views of the

Llanbister — note the slope

Beguildy

Ithon valley below, reinforcing the need in former times to regard a church not only as a place of worship but also as a strong point in the defence of the neighbourhood. The additional fact that the church is set in an immense circular churchyard emphasises the great age of this religious settlement. The church is dedicated to St Cynllo, a sixth century Celtic missionary. Celtic missionaries like Cynllo established Christianity in Radnorshire in monastic cells; such a one was built in the sixth century here in Llanbister, which became the mother house for other cells in the district. The roundness of the huge churchyard, along with the proliferation of yew trees, prompts the usual query concerning a possible pre-Christian settlement on the site, especially as there is nearby a well whose supply of water has never been known to fail, but as often in these circumstances there is no archaeological evidence to support the theorising.

However there is documentary evidence which underlines the social significance of the festivities associated with the local patronal day, which was observed on the 17th of July. On the first Sunday after that date most parishoners flocked to service to remember St Cynllo in church before taking to the churchyard where they remembered him in a more boisterous fashion. By the nineteenth century the eating and the drinking and the subsequent merrymaking in the churchyard seems to have got well out of hand, a tendency which succeeding vicars were not able to correct for long, although one incumbent in the 1820s prayed with such passion for a thunderstorm that for that year at any rate the jollification was completely washed out! Great quantities of ale, brewed under the orders of the churchwardens, were carried by eager volunteers into the churchyard, upon whose walls were stacked large pans of a local delicacy, reserved for the special occasion, which basically seems to have been a rice pudding, made solid by the addition of as many raisins as could be afforded! Every year the churchwardens decided which houses in the village should be entrusted with the task of preparing this essential part of the celebrations. The eating and the drinking (of cider as well as of beer) were usually followed by churchyard games and widespread dancing, which was a general feature of patronal celebrations in Radnorshire right up to the end of the nineteenth century.

Casgob — on a mound

Three miles south of Llanbister leave the A483 at the village of Llanddewi Ystradenni and go by country roads through Dolau to Llanfihangel Rhydieithon (GR 152668), whose church, fittingly dedicated to St Michael, looms over the A488. A brief walk through the hilly churchyard, behind which broods the Radnor Forest, will reveal more Radnorshire mid-nineteenth century gravestones of excellent quality. Opposite the churchyard gate is a stone building, which formerly housed the village school. It bears a plaque, indicating that thanks to the generosity of local freeholders and other parishoners a school was opened here in 1848 (twenty two years before the 1870 Education Act).

Back on to the A488, where after another three miles another short stop is suggested to look at the church and churchyard at Bleddfa (GR 217684), where in the round and raised churchyard there is a thirteenth century church, to which a tower was added in the following century. Later it collapsed, doing much damage to the nave. Excellent restoration and renovation this century have produced an unusual and an impressive church. The churchyard which has had no burials on the north side has a few table tombs and some well-carved nineteenth century slabs.

This excursion ends on a high note by visiting the church and churchyard at Casgob (GR 239664); to get there, leave the A488 at Monaughty, turn right on to B4356, turn right again at Whitton, and after a mile and a half right yet again up a country road, signposted Casgob 2 miles. This road is marked by a clump of Scots pines at the intersection; until 1767, when the Turnpike Trust saw fit to do some drastic re-routing hereabouts this cul-de-sac to Casgob was part of the Great Road, which ran from London through to Aberystwyth. Today Casgob is really remote, not being on the road to anywhere; the hamlet consists of the church, a farm and the former school, with room for parking next to the telephone kiosk outside the churchyard gate. The churchyard is round and very large; it is likely that men and women lived there before the building of the first Christian church but whether these first settlers were Bronze Age people or Christian refugees from Roman Britain, it seems impossible to know at this distance of time. When the strong arm of Roman protection was withdrawn at the beginning of the fifth century many groups moved westwards, seeking the security of the hills. If, as seems likely, such people came this way, they will probably have settled in this place. The churchyard is so extensive that after a wet spring and early summer, it is almost impossible to penetrate beyond the church tower at the western end where all around is a tangle of bramble and willow herb and bracken. The church is built on high land and is dedicated to St Michael, not surprisingly as the Radnor Forest is close by to the west; its stout western tower seems to have been built into a large mound, which was probably thrown up to offset the sort of structural weakness of the tower, that did such damage at Bleddfa.

On the north wall of the nave hangs a framed parchment, which was dug up some years ago in the churchyard, where originally it was deliberately buried. It is an Abracadabra charm, dating from 1700, specifically designed to drive out evil spirits that were thought to be besetting a parishoner, Elizabeth Lloyd. It is a splendid mixture of Christian and pagan ideas, couched in English and dog Latin. Jesus Christ, "who caused the blind to see, the lame to walk and the dumb to talk" is invoked along with Adonais. Added interest is given to the charm by some of the phrases which had been lifted wholesale from the writings of the famous Elizabethan mathematician and astrologer, Dr John Dee, whose family home was at Nant-y-groes, scarcely more than two miles from Casgob.

The churchyard today is mostly bounded by hedges, but it looks as if originally there was a high earthen rampart which would have given some measure of protection to those who had built their huts there. Of the many surviving yew trees by far the largest and oldest is the one just south-west of the church tower. It is pleasing to note that the men and women of the parish still like to mark notable events by planting trees. Twice this century coronations have been commemorated by the planting of trees, which are to be found, suitably labelled, in the north-east part of this historic churchyard.

C. East of the Wye

This second part of the churchyard survey of old Radnorshire comprises two groups, one in the pleasant pastoral country around Llandrindod Wells, the other south of Builth Wells up the Edw Valley, climbing on to the wild uplands that finally merge into the Radnor Forest. Of the seven churchyards to be visited, all have points of special interest but three of them are of considerable historical importance, those at Diserth (*Disserth*), Aberedw and at Rhulen (*Rhiwlen*).

Cefnllys church (GR 084615) is only two miles east of Llandrindod Wells but is by no means easy to find; leave the town along Cefnllys Lane, which gradually leaves behind all houses as it drops down to the river Ithon at a delectable spot, called Shaky Bridge, besides which is a Nature Reserve and a capacious picnic site. The only building to have survived in this once well-populated area is St Michael's church, to reach which it is necessary to cross the bridge and follow the track around the flank of Cefnllys Hill until the church becomes visible down below between the hill and the river. This church served a considerable population in the Middle Ages but today stands alone, above a field, whose frequent undulations indicate the sites of former dwellings; today its sole protection comes from an impressive circle of yew trees, which mark the boundaries of the churchyard.

All human life seems now to have left this beautiful stretch of the Ithon, which probably from the Bronze Age had witnessed a great deal of human activity. The hill on which the church was built, may have been first settled by Bronze Age people; certainly later on an Iron Age fort was established on Cefnllys Hill, the ramparts of which were used by the Normans when they put up a motte and bailey there soon after the Conquest and again in the thirteenth century when the Mortimers erected a stone castle on the hill. By 1300 this castle dominated the valley, with the people who supplied the needs of this military stronghold living down below in the meadows surrounding the church. This planned medieval town flourished briefly in the fourteenth century but had failed by 1400. Two centuries later

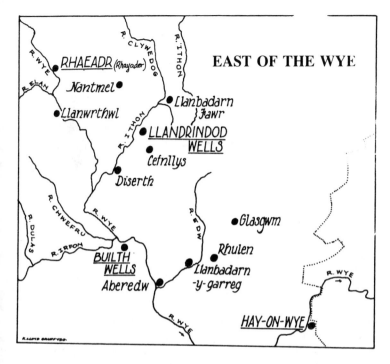

EAST OF THE WYE

Camden visiting Cefnllys, commented "a lonely ruin". In 1832 parliamentary commissioners decided that the sparse population no longer merited the right to choose their own Member of Parliament! The final blow fell in 1893, when the Archdeacon of Llandrindod ordered the roof of the church to be removed to compel the few remaining worshippers to attend the newly-built church at Llandrindod. The ploy failed, however, and enraged public opinion saw to it that a new roof was put in position two years later. Today an enthusiastic band of Christians has succeeded in stirring up considerable interest in this fine old church with the result that services there at least in the summer months are well attended. The studious and the imaginative will derive great satisfaction from a leisurely afternoon spent in this idyllic little valley.

On the A483 one mile north of Llandrindod Wells is the church of Llanbadarn Fawr (GR 643088), with a convenient car

113

park on the other side of the road. A brief stop here is suggested both to view the thick circle of yews which provide the boundary to the churchyard, whose medieval church was destroyed in the rebuilding of 1878, and also to admire the tympanum in the south doorway, which represents the final artistic fling of the great school of Herefordshire craftsmen in the twelfth century.

Nantmel (GR 034663) is situated just above the A44 five miles south-east of Rhaeadr; it is a very ancient site, having been first consecrated in the sixth century by the same St Cynllo, who was the founding father of the church at Llanbister. The church, mostly rebuilt in the eighteenth century, is set on a hill, in a circular churchyard, and is approached by twelve broad and steep stone steps; the churchyard, which is very well looked after, has a semi-circle of yew trees on the south and south-east sides and a number of good eighteenth century gravestones, following the strong local tradition.

A mile to the west of Llandrindod on the road to Builth, the A483, is a right hand turning, on to a minor road, which in a mile leads to Diserth (GR 034583), whose white church will be seen nestling in the valley below the hill; just before the bridge is reached, which spans the Ithon, turn left down a short cul-de-sac, which gives access after a hundred yards to the church and a farm, behind which members of the Caravan Club have their pitches beside the river. The church and the farm today comprise Diserth, the most likely derivation of whose name is the Latin desertum, meaning a secluded place and therefore a most suitable location for a hermitage, which was the nature of the earliest ecclesiastical settlement here. In this hermitage lived St Cewydd, a sixth century Christian missionary, who from his headquarters here in a wooden church in a circular llan moved out and about to try to convert to Christianity any man or woman in the district whom he could persuade to stop and listen.

St Cewydd's round churchyard survives but the church it circles dates from the thirteenth century, the entrance to which is through a south door on the far side of the church from the lane. Much building and rebuilding went on in the succeeding centuries but what makes Diserth church unique among the churches of Radnorshire is that it alone escaped restoration in the nineteenth century, so that the church the visitor enters today looks exactly as it did three hundred years ago, its atmosphere unmistakably that of the seventeenth century. It is a fascinating place.

St Cewydd's patronal day was celebrated on the second Sunday in July (the observance has recently been revived). In 1744 a Shropshire lawyer on holiday happened to visit Diserth in July. Happily he wrote down all that he saw; his report which survives furnishes us with an invaluable eye-witness account of social life at the time. First he came upon a man leading a horse, which was pulling a sledge, bearing a cask of ale. The man was delivering it, he said, to Diserth Wake, some two miles away. On arrival at Diserth the lawyer had to make his way through a crowded lane to get to the churchyard, which was thronged with people dancing to the music provided by a fiddler, seated on a table-tomb. In a nearby barn, which, he thought, was reserved "for people of fashion and fortune", he saw nine couples enjoying themselves in a dance. The farm opposite the churchyard gate was until 1897 licensed as a public house, which played a central part in these festivities, catering for the needs of those who in the wide open spaces in the churchyard were playing all manner of games, the most popular of which seems to have been a primitive form of tennis and fives. All in all, here in Diserth the patronal saint was well remembered. Dancing and the playing of fives in the churchyard at Diserth — and not only during the patronal festivities — continued there until little more than a hundred years ago.

Today Diserth churchyard has changed but little; the north side, where goats now graze, is still a green pasture, as it was when the patronal revels took place, but on the south side there are graves everywhere, a number of interesting table tombs catching the eye. Burials today are at the west end of the very large churchyard where much of the dancing used to take place. Time seems to be standing still in Diserth, especially in the winter months, when the caravans on the bank of the lovely river are no longer occupied.

Aberedw (GR 080474) is on the east bank of the Wye, six miles south of Builth at a point where the mountain stream Edw joins forces with the Wye, after forcing its way through a gorge. The Edw valley is one of the least known but most beautiful valleys in the whole of Wales; to those who know the district Aberedw is famous for its rocks, the remains of Llywelyn the Last's stone castle and the cave nearby, where circumstances forced him to hide until one morning in 1282, when he left his hiding place for the last time and strode down to Aberedw church, where he celebrated mass, before going to his death in a skirmish near Builth. Aberedw's church, standing above the river Edw, though much restored in the nineteenth century, has many features, including the nave, which hark back to the fourteenth century. It is dedicated to St Cewydd, a fact which rightly suggests some connection with Diserth, from which base the early Celtic missionary succeeded in winning enough converts in the Edw Valley to set up a llan there in which he built Aberedw's first place of worship, a flimsy affair of wood and wattle. Another and much later connection with Diserth was provided in the eighteenth century when the same Shropshire lawyer who visited Diserth during the patronal festivities in July, had gone on there after participating in a similar happy jollification the previous month in Aberedw.

At Aberedw the entrance to the church (the key to which can be obtained from the public house next door) is — unusually — on the north side; the churchyard, south of the church near the river, is filled with graves, whereas until recent times the north side, which remained unconsecrated in the Middle Ages, was mostly an open space, apart from its trees, the two most significant of which, yews, near the porch, cover so much ground that according to local tradition sixty couples have been known to dance beneath its spreading limbs. The Shropshire lawyer, visiting in the middle of the eighteenth century, witnessed the dancing under the trees but added that "the quality danced in an erection made of twigs and branches". He also commented on, as did other visitors, the use to which the stout walls of the tower were put, namely for enthusiastic games of fives.

From the point of view of the social historian perhaps the most notable feature of the church at Aberedw is the porch, which in the heyday of the Middle Ages often played a very important

Diserth — goats grazing in churchyard

Rhulen — the hidden jewel of old Radnorshire

117

role in local life. Certainly a great number of secular activities were associated with this particular porch, whose double tiers of stone benches are fourteen feet long. Here the musicians played to accompany the dancing under the yew trees and elsewhere in the churchyard. In addition in this porch itinerant merchants were allowed, when the weather was bad to sell their wares, while the parish council regularly conducted their business in this most public of places. Perhaps the last word about Aberedw should be allowed to the diarist Kilvert, who walked there over the hills one May morning, from Clyro (*Cleirwy*), which in later years he nostalgically called to mind with the heart-felt comment "Oh Aberedw, Aberedw!" It has changed but little in the past one hundred and twenty years.

Moving eastwards from Aberedw up the narrow Edw Valley, the road after two and a half miles crosses over to the south bank of the stream; before the bridge is crossed park the car in the available space at one side of the bridge and walk across to where the single-cell, white-washed church of Llanbadarn-y-garreg (GR 113487) beckons. St Padarn, a contemporary of St David, was popular in these parts as this is the third church so dedicated to be visited in Powys. This primitive thirteenth century church stands in a field beside the Edw; it is a peaceful, pastoral scene, with an ancient yew mounting guard over the entrance gate.

In the wildest and least accessible part of the Radnorshire Hills is an early Christian settlement at Rhulen (*Rhiwlen*), which is not particularly near anywhere. After leaving Llanbadarn-y-garreg continue on the same road for another two miles and then turn right to an even more minor road. A short distance along this road turn left on to a very narrow road indeed labelled Rhulen, which is about half a mile away. There is no obvious passing place, but as there is only one farm along this lonely road, the risk is worth the taking, especially as the reward is great. The small white church will eventually be seen on top of a bank on the right-hand side. To the privileged few who manage to get this far, Rhulen is a very special place to which man and nature have together made significant and complementary contributions. As far as the eye can see there are rounded hills, remote and largely uninhabited. To the south a drover's route climbed over Rhulen

Hill, avoiding its many dangerous peat pools, on its way to Painscastle (*Llanbedr Castell-paen*). Kilvert, who, when curate at Clyro, frequently roamed these hills, only once made any specific reference to Rhulen and then merely to record that a horrific murder had taken place there. Below the church at the bottom of the hill are two or three houses, comprising all that remains of a once more populous place. At the beginning of the nineteenth century there was an inn, the Cross Keys, while in the 1847 census the parish had a population of a hundred and twenty-nine, which by 1901 had dwindled to fifty-nine. Today there are fewer than thirty people in the parish.

The first people to live on the mound on which church and churchyard today stand were probably of the Bronze Age; when two thousand years later, in the sixth century a Christian clas was established at Glasgwm, about four miles away, the Celtic missionaries, operating from there, set up two mission stations, one of which was at Rhulen. This llan probably comprised no more than a flimsy hut, where a monk lived and prayed and catered for the needs of such local converts as he had made. This

Aberedw — note the large porch.
Between the two yews the villagers danced

119

church at Rhulen, like the parent house at Glasgwm, was dedicated to St David who is credited in local folk-lore with having in person made the very first Christian connection in this area.

The present church was built on the same site in late Norman times, two external features at once catch the eye. The west wall leans, though not at such an alarming angle as it did before the highly-skilful rebuilding of the wall in 1988, and the east wall is threatened by the roots of a very large old yew, whose bulk even in the fourteenth century was sufficient to prevent any extension being made to the chancel. Entrance to the church is through a porch on the south side, on the seventeenth century door of which there still survives a sanctuary ring. In springtime the churchyard is a golden field of daffodils. The relatively few graves, all of which are well-tended, occupy only a very small part of the churchyard. The trees, mostly yews, are huge and ancient, the one just east of the chancel, which had prevented any extension in former times, crashed a few years ago and had to be felled, though of course its roots remain. The walls of the church are thick, the door set into a shouldered recess, a most unusual shape, which is repeated in the recess behind the altar. Plain and unadorned, this church, set in this peaceful churchyard, has an ambience all its own; by some mysterious alchemy it adds up to more than the sum total of its constituent parts.

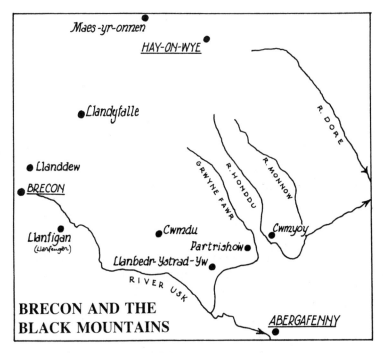

Maes-yr-onnen
HAY-ON-WYE

Llandyfalle

Llanddew
BRECON

R. DORE

GRWYNE FAWR
R. HONDDU
R. MONNOW

Llanfigan
(Llanfeugan)

Cwmdu
Partrishow
Llanbedr-Ystrad-Yw

Cwmyoy

RIVER USK

**BRECON AND THE
BLACK MOUNTAINS**

ABERGAFENNY

D. Brecon and the Black Mountains

The fourth and last part of the Powys survey concerns itself
with Brecknockshire, which covers a very large area indeed,
much of it mountains and valleys, and contains a great many
interesting and ancient churchyards, of which five have been
chosen to represent the rest. Of these two are in the Brecon area,
one to the north of the county town and the other to the south
near the river Usk under the Brecon Beacons, while the other
three are much further south in the Black Mountains north of
Abergavenny (*Y Fenni*).

Though Llan-ddew (GR 055308) is only two miles north of
Brecon, it lies well away from main roads in an elevated and
really remote position. The village church, the oldest in the old
county of Brecknockshire, still seems, despite repeated, though
sensitive restoration, basically to belong to the Middle Ages; it
stands in a nearly round churchyard, near the south door of

121

which eight larch trees were formerly planted to give the church much-needed protection from the prevailing south-westerly wind. The recent felling of four of these stalwarts provoked much local controversy. Where the visitor now lingers, assimilating the peaceful atmosphere of all about, there was an early llan, in which a small church, presumably of wood, was built before 500; this fact is known because there is a record that an unfortunate princess of Powys took refuge in this church in that year. Later more substantial building on the same site made possible the setting up of a clas, which performed its ecclesiastical and educational duties until the early part of the twelfth century. The supply of water essential for such communal life was provided by the well that still pours forth a generous supply of water across the lane from the churchyard. The present church, begun in the twelfth century, acquired a distinguished near neighbour in 1175, when Giraldus Cambrensis was appointed to the office of Archdeacon of Brecon, necessitating him taking up residence in the so-called Bishop's Palace, under whose garden wall the all-important well was sited.

Giraldus approved of his new home which, he thought, was "well adapted to literary pursuits and the contemplation of eternity"; the immediate task he set himself was to improve the moral standards of the clergy under his care. Evidence of his zeal has already been seen over the rededication of the church in Kerry in 1176. In his own archdiaconate he reacted so vigorously to clerical misdemeanours at Llanbadarn Fawr, near Llandrindod Wells that when he visited the area his retinue was greeted with a shower of arrows, which caused the Archdeacon to take shelter in the church, where he was for a time besieged. Busy though Giraldus was in the affairs of state and the enrolment of volunteers for the Third Crusade, he never relented in his attempt to stop his clergy from revelling with their parishoners in churchyard festivities, revelling that sometimes, he discovered, followed patronal services in the church where cider had been substituted for communion wine! The palace of Giraldus is no more; the ruined site was built upon in 1867 to provide a home for the vicar, but the garden wall still stands under which the well continues to serve the needs of the parish.

Five miles south-east of Brecon on the B4558 above the river Usk is the village of Pencelli, where once the crossing of the Usk was protected by a stone castle, put up in the thirteenth century by Ralph de Mortimer. Half a mile west of Pencelli in the eastern foothills of the Brecon Breacons is the church of Llanfigon (*Llanfeugan*, GR 086245), which was built by the same Ralph de Mortimer in 1272. Intending visitors to Llanfigon are advised to enquire in Pencelli for directions to the church, as the lane to it bears no sign-post. There can be few more suitable or more attractive sites for a church than the one on which Mortimer chose to build, though in fact it had first been chosen and built upon by early Christians many centuries before. The churchyard is round and raised up and very extensive; its circumference is marked out by twelve very large yew trees, the two biggest of which — and therefore the oldest — being in the north-eastern part of the churchyard.

On the south side survive the base and the shaft of a medieval churchyard cross; the far side of the churchyard, for many years unconsecrated, where now birdsong abounds in the overgrown trees, once rang with the raucous shouts and excited cries of parishoners at play. The stout walls of the tower, which is at the western end of the church, were much in demand for ball games until the middle of the nineteenth century, (the three horizontal string courses of stone must have come in very useful), while in the north-east corner of the churchyard, near the two massive yew trees, there was once a cockpit.

Readers may like to be reminded of the associations in this neighbourhood with St Illtud, which were briefly mentioned when the church, dedicated to him at Llanelltud near Dolgellau, was being described. Llanhamlach, where the missionary spent some time as a hermit, lies a mile to the north of Pencelli across the Usk, Giraldus Cambrensis, who loved a story, related that while St Illtud was living as a hermit near Llanhamlach, "the mare which used to carry his provisions to him became gravid after being covered by a stag, and gave birth to a creature, which could run very fast, its front part being like that of a horse and its haunches resembling those of a deer." A traveller's tale indeed!

For full enjoyment of the ancient and beautiful churchyard at

Cwm-du (GR 181238) a sunny day is desirable; it is superbly situated just off the A479 on the west side of the Black Mountains above the river Rhiangoll, which two miles further south flows past Tretower (*Tretŵr*) to merge into the Usk after another mile. The church is built on a considerable mound, and is, not surprisingly, dedicated to St Michael. According to the Book of Llandaf (the *Liber Landavensis*), a twelfth century inventory of church lands, this church was consecrated in 1060 by the Bishop of Llandaf, along with the next two churches to be visited, at Llanbedr Ystrad Yw and at Partrishow (*Patrisio*). In all three cases, the new churches were made of stone and at Cwm-du and at Llanbedr replaced earlier and presumably wooden buildings; in all probability too both dedications were changed. New patronal saints were chosen who would not give offence to Norman susceptibilities!

The churchyard is very large indeed and round, its boundaries established by more than twenty full-grown yew trees. Whether early man had settled there in the Bronze Age is not known but the likelihood that early Christians set up a llan here centuries before the stone church was built is increased by the survival of two early Christian memorial stones. In a buttress in the south wall between the church porch and the priest's door is the first stone which was obviously built into the wall at a much later date. The inscription is in Latin and in Ogham characters and commemorates the death in the sixth century of one Catacus, the son of Tegernacus; the other surviving stone stands against the wall in the little porch in front of the priest's entrance door. This too is inscribed in Latin and is thought to be of slightly later date; it is decorated with a ringed cross. South of the church in a prominent position are the remains of a medieval churchyard cross of which the base and part of the shaft survive.

Llanbedr Ystrad Yw (GR 239205) probably owes its existence to its geographical position at the foot of the valley down which the Grwyne Fechain hurries on its way to join the Usk below Crickhowell, which is named after the Iron Age fort, Crug Hywel, which lies above Llanbedr to the east. There was probably an early Christian settlement here but the first church for which there is any documentary evidence is the stone building

Llanfigan (Llanfeugan) — shaft

Cwmdu — sun-dial

referred to in the Book of Llandaf as having been consecrated in 1060. The present church mostly dates from the fifteenth century, though the tower is older and part of the nave may have survived from the eleventh century building. Certain it is that men and women have worshipped here for at least eight hundred years, to which the presence in the churchyard of four very large and therefore ancient yew trees bears testimony. As so often in Welsh churches, built before the Reformation, there stands in the churchyard, as witness of the past, the remains of a churchyard cross, mutilated by royal decree in the sixteenth century; only the original base now remains, though part of the shaft was at one time renewed to hold a sundial, which too has now disappeared.

There are reminders too in the churchyard of the times when the Welsh Sunday was a lively day of bodily as well as of spiritual exercise and refreshment, when churchyards rang, outside the hours of divine service, with the happy sounds of people enjoying themselves. On the outside wall of the north chancel can be seen holes in the fabric in which iron hinges had once been secured to protect the precious glass against the balls struck too hard by eager fives' players. A similar situation has already been mentioned in this book, at Llandyfalle, near Llan-ddew, north of Brecon, where ball games in the churchyard continued well into modern times. On his first visit to Llandyfalle, the author, having exclaimed at seeing the hinges still in place in the wall, found in the long grass actual pieces of the shutters. At Llanbedr it is known that action against the players was taken in 1785, when the Rector ordered the churchwardens "to curb this nuisance", whereupon shutters were made and put in place. Before leaving Llanbedr notice should also be taken of the porch, which is older than most, having been added in the fifteenth century; since then it has played over the centuries a significant part in the secular as well as in the religious life of this parish.

There is no village at Partrishow but a visit to the church and churchyard (GR 279224) should be thought of as a pilgrimage; pilgrims, if they are of the right calibre, must be patient and be prepared to endure hardship, though, if Partrishow be approached on foot, nothing is to be expected worse than a steep

Partrishow — in the background the cross where Archbishop Baldwin preached

walk and frequent stops to consult the Ordnance Survey map! Most modern pilgrimages however are made by car and in this case, preferably by small car, as the steep lanes are very narrow. Though Partrishow lies four and a half miles north-east of Crickhowell, the easiest route to take is via the A465 Abergavenny to Hereford road, turning left into the Honddu Valley at Llanfihangel Crucornau. After a mile and a half turn left again at a telephone kiosk and continue on this minor road in a westerly direction for two miles until there is a meeting of five lanes. Go straight across a stone bridge, which is known as the Bishop's Bridge, because Archbishop Baldwin in the company of Giraldus Cambrensis passed that way in the twelfth century. Soon a T-junction is reached; turn right here and change gear!

After a mile the road widens and flattens, allowing a car to be parked on the grass on the left hand side. Ahead up another steep but short hill may be glimpsed the church but first walk across the lane and look for the well on the other side. Without this well there would have been no Partrishow, church or churchyard. It has to be said that for once there is no known prehistoric association with this well.

Tradition has it that in the sixth century Issui, a Celtic missionary, settled in a hut by this well, where he began his mission of preaching, converting and healing the sick, a mission that became so successful that after his untimely death at the hands of a sick man whom he had healed, his healing powers were transferred in the public mind to the well itself, which thereafter acquired a considerable reputation for healing the sick. Five centuries later, in the eleventh century, a wealthy leper came that way, and was healed by the soothing waters of the well; in gratitude he built a church on the top of the hill, at a height of fifteen hundred feet, dedicating it to the memory of this Celtic saint Issui. This is the church which, according to the Book of Llandaf, was built in 1060. There is parking space for two cars outside the lych gate which gives access to the lonely church, whose treasures include an eleventh century font, stone altars, bearing six consecration crosses and a wonderful late fifteenth century screen, but only the font survives from the original church.

In the churchyard, beyond the ancient yews will be found quite close to the south wall of the nave a medieval preaching cross in its entirety, apart from a twentieth century calvary. Happily it escaped truncation at the hands of government commissioners in the sixteenth century, because they were unable to find their way to Partrishow. The same remoteness also saved the consecration crosses from being defaced. Archbishop Baldwin is said to have preached the Third Crusade from the steps of this cross in the presence of the ever-faithful Giraldus Cambrensis and a group of local Christians who were gathered on the stone seats that run around the outside of the south wall. As the visitor reluctantly leaves this special place, he should notice, west of the church, a small stone building, where in former days the officiating priest stabled his horse.

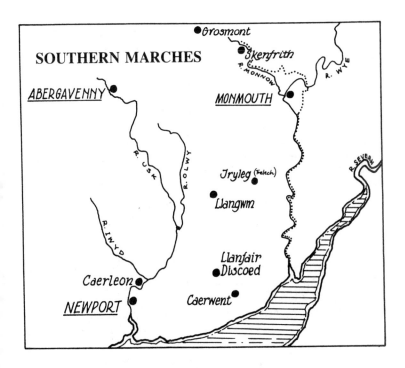

3. GWENT AND GLAMORGAN

A. The Southern Marches

If only boundaries were logically drawn, the next churchyard to be seen would have followed the visit to Partrishow from which it is separated by only two miles, as the buzzard travels. However Cwmyoy (*Cwm-iou*, GR 299233) is in Gwent and therefore has to appear as a foreword to the section on Gwent rather than more appropriately as a postscript to Powys. Visitors to Partrishow, on their way back, may care to continue up the Honddu Valley for a short distance before crossing the river and going up to Cwmyoy, which is perched high up on a spur above the valley. Christianity was first brought to the Honddu Valley in the sixth century, possibly by St David himself, though there is no surviving trace of early Christian settlement in Cwmyoy, which from the time that the Augustinian priory of Llanthony (*Llanddewi Nant Hodni*) was established a few miles further up the valley received its clergy from that monastery.

Today's visitors will soon see the uniqueness of Cwmyoy, as it has only narrowly escaped destruction in one of the many landslips that have occurred in the neighbourhood. The western tower has heavily leaning walls, which have been stoutly buttressed against any further movement, while the chancel has lurched in a different direction. In 1871 a medieval cross was dug up in a local farmyard and later placed in the nave of the church from which it was stolen in 1967. Today it is happily back in the church, having been discovered in an antique shop in London! In the churchyard, where in the eighteenth century the great Methodist pioneer George Whitefield preached, at the invitation of the vicar, who had a sympathetic interest in what Hywel Harris was doing, there are gravestones of outstanding quality as there were in the valley in the past a number of exceptionally talented stonemasons.

By Southern Marches, however, is really meant that pleasant, peaceful area that lies west of the Monnow and west of that part of the Wye that flows south from Monmouth to Chepstow; where today anglers, walkers and historically-minded people find so much enjoyment, in former times, and especially in the troubled times that followed the Norman conquest of England, it was potentially a battlefield and certainly for centuries the area was subject to military organisation. To the Normans Monmouth was all-important and in order to strengthen its position three castles were built to the north-west of the stronghold, which together were known as the Trilateral, but separately identified as White Castle, Grosmont and Skenfrith. The churchyards at Grosmont and at Skenfrith are the next to be viewed.

Grosmont (GR 404243), owing its existence to its geographical position on a hill, which gave the place its Norman-French name, came to the notice of the first Earl of Hereford in 1067, when he was looking for adequate protection for his new stronghold at Monmouth. The big hill, towering above the river Monnow, soon had a wooden castle on its summit, but by the beginning of the thirteenth century it had served its purpose and in 1201 King

John entrusted Hubert de Burgh with the task of rebuilding the castle in stone, proof of the importance of which can be found in the growth of a prosperous town to serve the needs of the castle. Although Grosmont today is no more than a large — and very attractive — village, the visitor may still see the bare bones of a spacious medieval town, which was cruciform in shape; from de Burgh's castle on the rock above the river the road ran down in a north-east to south-west direction to where in the thirteenth century St Nicholas' church was built. This non-Celtic dedication probably indicates that this was the first church to be built on that site. Certainly most of what is still visible in the church and churchyard dates from the same time as the stone castle. By 1400 Grosmont was at the peak of its importance; repeated and sometimes very successful Welsh raids had compelled the defenders to establish a very large garrison at Grosmont. Indeed on one occasion in the middle of the thirteenth century a surprise Welsh attack had resulted in the unceremonious escape in the middle of the night of Henry IV and Queen Eleanor in their night clothes! The church was obviously intended to hold many more people than it can ever hope to attract today — one must imagine compulsory church parades in what must have looked rather like a small cathedral.

In general in the Middle Ages, churches were built north of the settlements they served, access to the church being through a door on the south side after passing through the south side of the churchyard, which was consecrated ground; here at Grosmont however the position was reversed, as the castle on the hill to the north was built before the church, which had to be relegated to the site at the bottom of the hill, south of the main settlement. Thus the north part of the churchyard was consecrated, with the entrance to the church being through a north door; the capacious area behind the church, which since the Reformation has been much used for burying, in the Middle Ages was the place where the men of the garrison and their families disported themselves in a variety of secular activities.

Near the entrance gate in the northern consecrated part of the churchyard is an early medieval preaching cross, part of whose shaft remains, firmly secured and — unusually — into an octagonal base; it may be noted, though no known inference may be derived from the observation, that the stout tower of the church is likewise octagonal. The shaft was lopped in the sixteenth century, but curiously enough the carved capstone, which was later placed upon it, is definitely of medieval origin, although where it came from no-one knows.

The spiritual needs of Grosmont today are adequately catered for by the chancel, which in 1880 was partitioned off from the nave by a glass division. The high and commodious former nave, now deconsecrated, is part graveyard and part store room-cum-museum and is of considerable interest to the social historian. Memorial inscriptions abound and along the south-east wall will be found the Grosmont hutch, an early church chest, possessing four locks, and nearby a strange half-carved figure, whose unknown but much-guessed-at identity excites the interest of the curious.

Skenfrith (GR 457202), three miles south of Grosmont, had probably existed as a Celtic settlement long before the Normans passed that way; its name is Celtic in origin, the Welsh form being Ynysgynwreid, meaning 'the island of Cynwraidd', who is believed to have been a local Celtic chief. Today's village has the good fortune to be marooned on a minor road, though quite close to the B4521 and it faces the Monnow which is here the national boundary and a paradise for anglers. Here shortly after the Norman conquest of England a wooden motte was put up, as at Grosmont, to be succeeded by a stone castle, built about 1210 by the same Hubert de Burgh, after he had finished similarly fortifying Grosmont.

The village street of Skenfrith is parallel to the Monnow; between the Post Office and the river is the castle, in front of which is a wide, well-grassed area, where cars may be parked. Only a passing mention is here permissible about the castle, but at least it must be said that Skenfrith possesses an unpretentious but perfect outline of a thirteenth century castle to which nothing has since been added to blur the idea of what a small Marcher stronghold of those distant years really looked like.

A hundred yards beyond the castle but still on the bank of the Monnow is the church, which de Burgh caused to be built at the

Grosmont — octagonal cross and tower

Skenfrith — graves grouped west of the church

same time as the castle. The dedication to St Bridget poses a problem, Bridget being the Saxon form of the Celtic St Ffraid; it has to be presumed that local sentiment succeeded in overcoming the normal Norman choice of a Peter, a Michael or a Mary. The emblems of St Bridget, acorns and oak leaves, are much in evidence in the church, while over the church porch there is a very ancient stone carving of a female head, which tradition insists is a true likeness of the patron saint.

Overhanging the main entrance to the churchyard is an old yew tree, beyond which is revealed one of the most picturesque churches imaginable, at the west end of which is a huge tower, crowned by a pyramid-shaped cap; its walls, five feet thick, afforded protection to all who sought shelter there in an emergency. In the upper parts of the tower slits can be seen, which ensured that doves too were welcome as a potential source of fresh meat, when border raids drove the men and women of the parish into the church. Inside much of the history of the Trilateral is encapsulated; there are too individual treasures to be admired, of which the Skenfrith cope must take the palm.

The original plan had been for Skenfrith to become a prosperous town like Grosmont but it suffered from its position, lying between Grosmont and Monmouth. Hence it failed as a medieval town and became instead a delightful village. Although the separate parts of Skenfrith, church and castle and cottages, are interesting and arresting, it is when they are taken together and viewed against the background of the river that they take on something of a magic quality. It is an enchanting place, where the past sometimes seems more real than the present.

On the B4293, which runs down the west side of the Wye, south of Monmouth is Trelech (alternatively Tryleg or Trelleck, GR 500054). Men first settled here in the Bronze Age; later came the Romans and after them the Saxons. In the Middle Ages Trelech was the largest town in the county, which helps to explain the size of the church and churchyard, the latter covering nearly two acres. Trelech's most recent claim to fame is as the birthplace of Bertrand Russell.

Today the fortunate visitor may see evidence of a number of cultures, though he may be puzzled by the name given to the oldest surviving landmark; for the three tall stones, which explain the name of the village, were raised for an as yet unknown reason by the people of the Bronze Age and are known as Harold's Stones, bearing anachronistic testimony to the interest taken in the district by the last Saxon King of England, some two and a half thousand years after the men of the Bronze Age settled in the area!

Trelech's handsome church, dedicated, like Grosmont's, to St Nicholas, gives house room to a curious treasure indeed, brought inside presumably for protection from the elements, a sundial, dated 1689, which commemorates in carving the Bronze Age alignment, a Norman motte and a medieval well, with the accompanying assurance in Latin that Harold had gained the victory! Pride of place in the churchyard, which is believed to be on the site of a Roman station, must go to a preaching cross, south of the main entrance to the church; it is referred to as pre-Norman and it may well be Saxon but what is perhaps of greater interest to many people is the likelihood that the actual place where the cross was erected may be the very spot where the first wooden cross was set up to mark the establishment of the first Christian llan in Trelech. These first Christian missionaries, who came here in the sixth or seventh century are likely to have baptised their converts with water taken from the nearby well, now known as the Virtuous Well, which was formerly St Anne's Well. The Bronze Age people whose alignment has already been referred to probably used this same well as their main water supply long before the Christians sanctified it and turned it to new uses.

Immediately south of the churchyard cross is a puzzle in stone, the church notes hinting "by the south side of the cross stands what might be a Druidical altar in stone". This stone "altar" is five feet long and two feet wide and stands on stone supports; just south of it is a stone slab, set in the ground, whose dimensions are about five feet by two. In the total absence of firm fact a reasonable surmise may be made that it is considerably older than the cross and pagan in origin. If this theory is correct, then the faint crosses carved on the north end of the "altar" may have been a Christian addition in after years to offset any lingering pagan influence it might be thought to have had in a Christian churchyard. Alternatively it may eventually be proved to be evidence of a Roman occupation of the site.

To round off this section on Gwent a churchyard has been chosen down a little-frequented lane, six miles to the east of Usk; Llangwm (GR 434006) is a quiet and peaceful place, not easy to find. In the village of that name turn east into a minor unsignposted lane behind the Bridge Inn. After half a mile the first of Llangwm's two churches will be seen in a field on the right. Continue on the road for another half mile until the second church appears, also on the righthand side, down a dell. Llangwm means "the llan in the dingle" and here in the seventh century the first Christian church was erected, of which, of course, there is now no trace. The present church was started in the thirteenth century and is dedicated to St Jerome, who was no Celtic missionary but rather a Christian scholar who spent most of his life in Italy. He became a zealous defender of the monastic way of life, prompting the thought that in early days this dell had its own monastic cell. The problem of the dedication deepens, however, when it is realised that in the two other Llangwms in Wales, one in Clwyd (GR 967447), the other in Dyfed (GR 990094), the dedication is to the same saint.

The large and circular churchyard, which has an unusual variety of trees, contains some excellent table tombs; there are also several arresting memorial inscriptions, two in particular, both from the mid-eighteenth century, belonging to the same Gwin family, catching the eye. The large seventeenth century tower is set north of the chancel to which it is joined by an arch. Despite extensive restoration in the middle of the nineteenth century much earlier work survives, including a magnificent late fifteenth century screen and rood loft. During the Victorian upheaval a stone, shaped like an hour-glass, was found built into the wall; this strange object now stands by the font and after much speculation has proved to be an early medieval lamp, which quite possibly constitutes the only material proof of an earlier building than the present church.

Trelech — a puzzle in stone

B. St Illtud Country

Churchyards already described have been chosen for a variety of reasons to do with such considerations as geographical position, historical association, relationship with particular events and localities; this churchyard at Llanilltud Fawr (*Llantwit Major*), though certainly worth inclusion for its situation and its associations, is rather more than that. It provides an occasion, metaphorically speaking, for taking off one's shoes. For, to those visitors to whom continuity of tradition and contact with early Christianity in Wales is meaningful, the ground is holy in the churchyard at Llanilltud Fawr, which has been transmogrified into Llantwit Major (GR 966687). It is a religious and historical site of outstanding importance. Llanilltud Fawr is situated close to the south coast of Glamorgan, about ten miles south of the M4 at Bridgend; to the historically minded the town has a great deal to offer over and apart from the church and churchyard. In addition it is an excellent centre for exploring an area, rich in scenery as well as in visual evidence of the past.

On the coast, less than a mile from Llanilltud Fawr, an Iron Age promontory fort, Castle Ditches (GR 960674) gives evidence of the first known settlement hereabouts; later came the Romans, who built for themselves a substantial villa, in the ruins of which, not so long afterwards, according to local tradition, Illtud lived for a while, when he arrived from Brittany at the end of the fifth century, before he set up a llan on the site of the present church and churchyard. This humble llan prospered so much that it became a clas, which, under Illtud's tutelage, blossomed into the most distinguished seminary of sound learning and religion in the whole of Wales. Jan Morris in *The Matter of Wales* refers to it as "one of the great international centres of Celtic Christianity, one of the chief instruments by which Roman and European traditions were cherished in Wales". Of its many well known alumni none were more famous than Cadog and Gildas, though even their intellectual stature was dwarfed by that of their master, Illtud. Tradition also claims that Patrick and Taliesin were educated there.

It is perhaps easier to understand the historical development

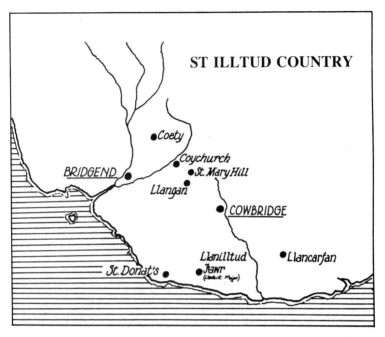

ST ILLTUD COUNTRY

of this famous but complicated site if the churchyard is first entered from behind the church on the seaward side; thus a little bridge has to be crossed, which spans the Afon Col-huw, a stream that will have supplied Illtud with the all important water which his little community needed, when the llan was first set up. No physical reminder remains of these very early days of primitive church, clas and monastic college; the very large building in the churchyard today is really an amalgamation of two churches, joined by a central tower. The eastern half, known as the 'new' church, was mostly built in the thirteenth century, while the western half, the 'old' church, is Norman in origin with fifteenth century additions. The 'old' church is a real store-house of the past, where there are displayed marvellous reminders of the early Celtic church, Christian crosses and memorial stones, brought in from the churchyard for protection; among them will be found a ninth century cross with a Latin inscription and two, slightly later, inscribed shafts of crosses.

Outside, on the south side is an impressive churchyard cross

139

and dotted about here and there among the many graves are the trunks of tall trees and some subtropical vegetation, while in a ruined building behind the western church growing very near the oil drum, which supplies the church with central heating, are tall teazles, to remind the visitor of industrious monks in the Middle Ages.

A two mile car journey westwards from Llanilltud Fawr leads to St Donat's (*Sain Dunwyd*, GR 934680); turn left in to what looks like a private road, which points to the fourteenth century castle, which today has become the Atlantic College. There is a public right of way to the church, which will soon be seen down a narrow cul-de-sac opposite the cliff on which the great building dominates the landscape. The mystery of the seemingly private road is dispelled by the knowledge that until the beginning of the twentieth century a public road ran close to the church until it was closed by the then owner of the castle.

The church and churchyard present an idyllic picture in the sheltered dell; it seems likely that fifteen hundred years ago, when Celtic missionaries travelled the western seas in their search for converts, they may well have sailed up the inlet, whose waters at that time washed the shore close to the bottom of today's churchyard. There was an early church on this site, dedicated to a Celtic missionary, St Gwerydd. When the Normans came to build there in the eleventh century, they changed the dedication to St Donatus; the church today, which dates mostly from the fifteenth century, retains a Norman arch in the sanctuary.

St Donat's today is wholly delightful — a Cotswold type church and churchyard near the sea! In addition it possesses on the south side of the churchyard a rare treasure, a fifteenth century churchyard cross; not only is the shaft complete but it is still capped by its original calvary. That it survives at all is remarkable, but its survival borders on the miraculous when it is remembered that during the Civil Wars in the seventeenth century Oliver Cromwell and a party of his Roundheads actually paid a visit to the castle on the hill above. Unfortunately what the soldiers spared, climatic conditions are now at work defacing. Grouped around the cross is a cluster of table tombs. The sense

Llanilltud Fawr (Llantwit Major)
— churchyard cross

St Donats —
cross under Atlantic College

Llangan — 9th c. cross

141

of timelessness imparted by the peaceful scene is heightened by the inscription to be found on a stone propped up in the porch. It reads "The following centenarians, in addition to those mentioned on other stones, have been buried in this churchyard. Francis Stych was buried December 1st 1671, aged 108 years. John Harry, of this parish, was buried May 24th 1792, aged 110 years (Extract from the Register of the parish)."

Cadog, while a student at Llanilltud Fawr with Illtud, became an outstanding Latin scholar as well as a man inspired with his master's missionary zeal. After leaving Illtud he too set up in the sixth century a monastic college, which was five miles to the east of Llanilltud Fawr at Llancarfan (GR 051702). Here Cadog's seminary not only trained missionaries who went out from there to spread the Gospel far and wide but also produced eminent scholars, who in these dark years did much to hold aloft the torch of learning. Every Lent, according to tradition, Cadog left Llancarfan and withdrew to the lonely island of Steep Holm, in the Bristol Channel (halfway between modern Barry and Weston-super-mare); in this same lonely island in the same sixth century another former leading light from Llanilltud Fawr, the historian Gildas took advantage of the solitude to write his famous diatribe on *The Decline of Britain*.

The inability of modern enquirers to find any trace of Cadog's monastic college in Llancarfan has been sensibly interpreted to mean that today's church and churchyard occupy the site. Llancarfan today still seems splendidly remote, although it is but two miles south of the busy A48; the church, which is in the very middle of the village, is delightfully situated in a hollow in a well-wooded valley, with a stream flowing past the churchyard under the Iron Age fort, Castle Ditches to the south-east. The church, which is, of course, dedicated to St Cadog, was started in Norman times and added to again and again in the Middle Ages; it has a very large churchyard indeed in which there are relatively few gravestones. The unconsecrated north side of the churchyard must have given much scope here for many secular activities in times past, a clue to which is provided by the survival in windows on the north side of gudgeons, which once held shutters, put up to protect the precious glass from straying balls!

Though there is perhaps not much to see in Llancarfan now, there is much to savour; it has an ambience all its own.

South east of Bridgend in the sparsely populated uplands in south Glamorgan, is the village of Llan-gan (GR 958778), in the outskirts of which, almost hidden from view in a grove of trees, is the very ancient village church, dedicated to St Canna. The north side of the churchyard has long since fallen into disuse and is now an almost impenetrable thicket of bramble but elsewhere in the churchyard there are two real treasures. The first of them, just south of the south porch, is a normal fifteenth century preaching cross, normal, that is, except that, as at St Donat's, it is complete. No parliamentary commissioners came that way to carry out the provisions of the law. Hence the calvary, carved in two tiers, is intact. The second treasure is an even more remarkable survivor; it is to be found west of the west door and is the carved head of a ninth century Celtic wheel-cross.

Halfway between Llan-gan and the M4 to the north, on high land, is the little church of St Mary Hill (GR 957794). (An Ordnance Survey map will save much time.) This is another very ancient foundation, much restored in Victorian times but in its elevated and windy churchyard is another preaching cross. The large, stepped base is the original one; the shaft is modern but it is capped by the original calvary, which is carved on all four sides. South Glamorgan is indeed fortunate to possess such crosses as those at St Donat's, Llan-gan and at St Mary Hill.

Coychurch (*Llangrallo*, GR 939798), which is two miles west of St Mary Hill, has been virtually caught up in the expansion of Bridgend; its thirteenth century church, standing in a very crowded churchyard, with a number of good yew trees, has an excellent tall medieval cross near the south door. An entry in the parish register speaks of a wedding ceremony in 1771, which had to be repeated a month later because the bridegroom had placed the ring on the wrong finger!

For a final visit in the Vale of Glamorgan Coety, two miles north-east of Bridgend (GR 924816) has been chosen; in the Middle Ages the village was dominated by a formidable combination of castle and church on the hill. The castle figured prominently in the life of South Wales from the twelfth to the eighteenth century when the estate was finally broken up. Today enough remains to attract the attention of holidaymakers, whose young children may safely be left in the playground, thoughtfully provided, by the local council, on the green below the castle. The church next door was built in the fourteenth century and from its churchyard the castle looms large and splendid; the churchyard itself is circular and has an ancient yew of considerable size, which flourishes on a small mound, around which there is a wall of stone a foot high. This hints at a pre-Christian occupation of the site, which is quite probable as early men settled in the district, the earliest evidence for which is provided by a neolithic long barrow about a quarter of a mile north of the church (Coed-parc-garw). On the south side of the churchyard, where there is the base of a medieval cross, there is much overcrowding of graves, in stark contrast to the north side where there are only three or four memorial stones. Inside the church there is a rarity, one of the very few surviving portable Easter Sepulchres, which dates from the middle of the sixteenth century.

Llangan — 15th c. cross   *St Mary Hill — churchyard cross*

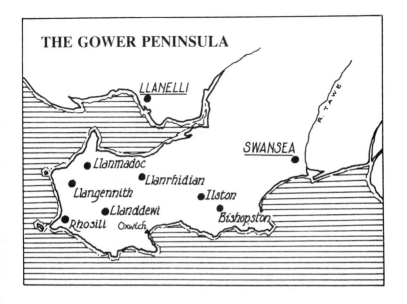

THE GOWER PENINSULA

LLANELLI

SWANSEA

R. TAWE

Llanmadoc
Llanrhidian
Llangennith
Ilston
Llanddewi
Bishopston
Rhosili   Oxwich

C. The Gower Peninsula

The Gower peninsula, like Anglesey, is an appendage of
Wales; those who live there share a common historical heritage.
Each area experienced considerable settlement in prehistoric
times and each was familiar with the tramp of Roman feet. The
centuries passed and some Christian missionaries crossed from
Ireland to set up their llans in Anglesey, while others came over
the sea from Brittany to make their first converts in the Gower.
Troubled times lay ahead when the Viking terror struck the
coasts of both exposed communities.

All these changes could be regarded as providing the
backcloth for what was to follow in the eleventh and succeeding
centuries when the victorious Normans sought to extend their
power westwards. In general terms the Normans settled in the
south of the peninsula, from which the Welsh were driven out to
exist as best they could in the north. Thereafter for several
centuries a prosperous trade grew up between south Gower and
the west country of England; this interchange of goods was
accompanied by the gradual settlement in the Gower of

immigrants from Somerset and Devonshire. Many a churchyard in the Gower today bears eloquent testimony to this infiltration of west country immigrants, in the gravestones of Tuckers, Groves and above all Mansells.

A clockwise tour of Gower churchyards is planned to start at Bishopston (GR 578894), which lies south-west of Swansea, from which it is still with some difficulty managing to keep its distance; the church is quite near the B4436 but pleasantly removed from its noise and bustle. In the southern part of today's churchyard, there flows a stream, near which the first Celtic missionary here, having thus found a suitable supply of water near at hand, built his flimsy, wooden hut, enclosed his llan and erected a wooden cross, which was to become thereafter a clear point of religious reference. The spot, hallowed by this wooden cross, in later years was marked by a cross of stone, whose base may still be seen near the south porch of the church. Today on this square base rests a round stone pedestal on the top of which there is a square hole in which in the Middle Ages a stone shaft stood up. The Book of Llandaf in the twelfth century makes reference to a church being established in Bishopston in about 480 to 490. If this fifth century date is accurate, the first church there will have been dedicated to some other Christian missionary than Teilo, who is the patron saint of today's church. (The Welsh name for Bishopston, it must be remembered, is Llandeilo Ferwallt.) Teilo, who was a contemporary of St David and who accompanied him on a pilgrimage to Rome and to Jerusalem, flourished in the middle of the sixth century.

The present church, which was begun in the twelfth to the thirteenth centuries, was sited on a very steep slope indeed, which presented succeeding generations with an enormous problem, as restoration and extension became necessary. It will be observed that very heavy buttressing has taken place on the north side of the church. The churchyard, which has had to be enlarged as the population of the parish has grown, has always been extensive and is noted for its fine old yew trees and its many well preserved eighteenth and nineteenth century gravestones.

Moving westwards first to Oxwich, whose churchyard has already been mentioned in connection with its holy well, then on to Rhosili (GR 417881), en route for a walk on Worms Head, provided that the month is other than August, when too many other people will have the same idea! There was probably an early Christian settlement at Rhosili but it will have suffered the same fate as that which befell the first stone church, which disappeared into the sand dunes in the fourteenth century. Today's church, built in the fourteenth century, to replace the one that was lost, has a distinctive saddle-back tower; mention has already been made of the sundial in the porch. The churchyard is very full of graves except for the south-west corner, which has no memorial stones at all. In 1830 disaster struck this coast and the dead sailors were given Christian but anonymous burial in this corner. Since that time other sailors, who have been similarly washed up on to this caring shore, have also been buried there. Another sailor, a Rhosili man, is commemorated in the church, on the north wall of the nave, Petty Officer Edgar Evans, who died with his master, Captain Scott, at the South Pole in 1912.

From Rhosili go back for three miles before turning left on to a road which a mile further on joins the A4418. Turn left on to this A road and continue on it for a while until it takes a right-angle to the right. At this point keep straight on — it becomes a minor road — pointing to Llanddewi. After passing Llanddewi church, with its saddle-back tower and rare medieval scratch dial, turn left again at Burry Green; after another two and a half miles Llangennith (*Llangynnydd*) will be reached (GR 428914). The visitor arriving here for the first time may be surprised to see a large village, complete with Post Office, shop, two inns and other amenities; he will be further surprised to realise that the road ends here, as Llangennith is not on the road to anywhere. Why then, the question must be asked, is there a community here at all? As always in such a situation concentrate on the church and churchyard, which face the green in the middle of the village.

History began in Llangennith in the sixth century, when a Christian missionary Cenydd, who appears to have been the only missionary to have been born in Gower, set up a llan and began to preach the Gospel. Legends abound about this holy man, but the only other hard fact known about him is that he was a contemporary of St David. From small beginnings this monastic cell at Llangennith flourished and became a clas until terror struck in the year 986 when the Vikings, having landed at the point, harried inland and utterly destroyed the clas and everyone who lived in and around it. Two hundred years of desolation followed before Christianity returned; a new monastery was then built and consecrated at the end of the eleventh or the beginning of the twelfth century. This priory consisted of modest monastic buildings, a small cloister, refectory, dormitory and equally modest outbuildings, though the priory church itself was very large and impressive. The monastery fell into disuse by the fifteenth century, when the priory church became today's parish church.

Behind the church today, and to the south-east of it, stands a large white house in whose garden piles of stones are thought to be vestigial traces of medieval monastic buildings; this is a private house, which was in former times a farmhouse, whose fields have now passed to a local farmer, who uses as a workshop a stone building that is actually joined on to the west end of the church. This is believed to have been the tithe barn of the monastery in the Middle Ages. Entrance to the churchyard is through a north gate; clearly because the monastic buildings were built south of the church, the north side of the churchyard had to be consecrated for burials, when the priory church became the parish church. Hence today the north side of the churchyard is the village burying place, where there are many old and interesting memorial stones. The east and south-east sides of the churchyard are very much overgrown, while there is no west or south-west side, because that area is occupied by the former tithe barn and the farmer's yard behind his workshop.

Across the narrow road in front of the north entrance to the churchyard is a well, which still flows freely; this indeed was a holy well, whose existence enabled St Cenydd to set up his llan where he did. As the centuries passed, the well came to supply the needs of the whole community, which it continued to do until the early years of the twentieth century. When main water was finally brought to Llangennith, all house-holders received letters, which advised them on no account to use the water from the well as it might well prove harmful!

148

Llangennith

Cheriton

149

This account of Llangennith began with St Cenydd and it seems only fitting that it should end with the patronal saint whose memory was always brought vividly to mind and cherished every year on July the fifth. On that patronal day, — and indeed on the two succeeding days as well — Llangennith remembered its founder in style, in celebrations which began in the church, spilled over into the churchyard and the village green, where dancing, all manner of games, and even boxing and cock fighting were much in demand. Nowhere in the whole of the peninsula was any patronal saint remembered in so boisterous a fashion and for so long as he was in Llangennith.

Llanmadog (GR 439935) is only a mile and a half north of Llangennith on foot, but is four miles away by road. A visit is recommended to those enthusiasts who are moved by the sight of an early Christian gravestone. One such, formerly in the churchyard at Llanmadog, is now safely lodged inside the little church. It is a sixth century memorial stone, commemorating in Latin one, Advectus, the son of Juanus.

From Llanmadog take the road past Cheriton church, whose saddle-back tower will be seen to the left of the road, until Llanrhidian (GR 497923) is reached, some four and a half miles east of Llanmadog. When in the first century BC the Celts of the Iron Age built themselves a large fort on the top of the hill to the east of Llanrhidian (Cilifor Top), they were overlooking the sea; indeed in the thirteenth century when the church was built, it was sited on a cliff-top, further to the east. Since then the silting up of the Burry has gone on apace, until today there are now miles of marshland between Llanrhidian and the sea.

The church, externally similar to the one at Cheriton, lies back from the village street, screened by tall trees; in its porch stands an ancient carved stone, known locally as the "Leper Stone", whose inscription has so far defied translation. The churchyard has a fine selection of gravestones, two of the most compelling being on the external south wall, the one dated 1646, the other 1746. The first one is the memorial stone of Robert Hary, who died in 1646 "who married two wives and had by them nine children". The epitaph reads thus:-

"Here lyeth my lifeless corps bereved of liveing breath
Not slaine by sinne which is the cause of death
But by decree which God hath said All Men Shall Dy
And Come to Judgement to know how they shall try.
And now, Heavenly God, That liveing breath Thou
gavest to Mee
That mortalle life and soule I yield and give againe to
Thee
My corps to earth for short time I doe give,
My soule unto my Saviour Christ eternally to live."

A few feet further to the west is the second stone, commemorating Agnes, wife of Samuel Morris, who died in November 1746, aged 27 years.

"Death with his dart hath pierc'd my heart
Whilst I was in my prime,
My husband dear, your grief forbeare,
Twas God's appointed time.
My tender husband dear, now cease to weep,
Death to the Saints is but an early sleep.
Go on Thro' Grace, in God's appointed way,
Then joyful shall we meet on the great day."
(At the bottom in capital letters)
AT THE EXPENSE OF SAMUEL MORRIS.

The path from the village street to the churchyard gate runs across a wide expanse of grass on both sides of which stand large lumps of limestone. Where they came from is a mystery as is the reason for their being sited just outside the churchyard gate. Local records state that in the middle of the nineteenth century one of them was moved to its present position by the initiative of the vicar and his churchwardens, who persuaded twenty strong young men of the parish to carry it. As the stone weighed two tons, the volunteers earned the pint of beer apiece, which they received for their trouble! Opposite the church is an old inn, happily still an hospitable one, which bears its unusual and time-honoured name, Welcome To Town, Gentlemen.

Ilston (*Llanilltud Gŵyr*, GR 558903), only a few miles inland from the Mumbles, has its church wonderfully situated in a well-wooded valley; dedicated to St Illtud, it possesses in the company of a number of other Gower churches, a saddle-back tower. It stands in a churchyard, which is graced by many large yews, the largest of which, close to the south door, grows out of a mound, which is surrounded by a wall three feet high. There is an abundance of eighteenth and nineteenth century tombstones, in addition to some well-preserved eighteenth century memorial slabs, which are propped up against the central tower. All in all, Ilston is a place of quiet beauty, much loved by the nineteenth century diarist, Kilvert, who several times stayed there at the rectory.

Llanddewi — medieval sun-dial on porch (above the lamp)

Mathri

St. Dogwells

Llandeloy

St. Non's

HAVERFORD
WEST

Llawhaden

Carew
Cheriton

PEMBROKE

TENBY

Penally

Manorbier

Basherton

4. DYFED

A. Around Haverfordwest

The church of St Nicholas at Penally (*Penalun*, GR 118992) is situated high up above the coast road, about two miles south-west of Tenby; in this neighbourhood St Teilo, the future companion of St David on pilgrimage, is believed to have been born, tradition also insisting that he died there too. The present church, built in the thirteenth century, is probably on the site of the original sixth century llan, with which it is quite possible that Teilo was connected. It certainly requires an imaginative approach today to recreate in the mind's eye the early days of Christian settlement in Penally, but help is at hand in the south transept of the church, where two churchyard crosses are now lodged for safety, crosses which a thousand years ago graced the

153

churchyard. The earlier of the two, probably put up in the second half of the ninth century, is about five feet high and is now without its cross, although it possesses an intricately-carved shaft; it was formerly sited in the north-east side of the churchyard. The other one, dating from the early tenth century, is a complete and richly-carved wheelhead cross; its original base is still visible in the churchyard, south-west of the west tower. The churchyard is hilly and extensive and contains some very large yews.

Four miles further west along the coast from Penally is Manorbier (GR 065976), where there is a sandy beach and a sheltered bay, above which on a cliff on the western side is the great castle of Manorbier, where Giraldus Cambrensis was born in 1146; on the east side on the opposite cliff stands out St James church. Giraldus was enthusiastic enough to write "Between the castle and the church a stream of water, which never fails, winds its way along an inlet. . . this is a region rich in wheat, with fish from the sea and plenty of wine for sale. . . In all the broad lands of Wales Manorbier is the most pleasant place by far." This exaggeration may be understood by the fortunate visitor who sits in the sun on the seat outside the churchyard gate and gazes across the inlet at the great man's house. Time seems to have stood still here, as in appearance castle and church are still very much as they were in the twelfth century, when the boy Giraldus had to cross the inlet in a hurry to find sanctuary in the church, when Tenby was being attacked.

Castle and church dominate the bay, the tall tower of the latter having in all probability been of inestimable use in troubled times in getting and giving advance warning of an enemy approach. The churchyard covers a wide area with the oldest gravestones to be seen south of the church. The walk from the churchyard gate to the church door is along a sunken passage, suggesting much overuse of this part of the churchyard for burying in the Middle Ages. St James — church and churchyard — today compete on equal terms with the famous castle; there can be few places, even in Wales, where the past and the present so overlap.

Inland between Tenby and Pembroke is Carew (*Caeriw*), famous for its cross, its castle and its church. The cross,

Manorbier churchyard

Carew Cheriton — Charnel House in churchyard

155

decorated with intricate, ornamental carving, towers fourteen feet above the side of the road; it belongs to the ninth century. Behind it is the castle, built in Norman times and much added to in later years, which became best known after the accession to the throne of England by Henry Tudor after the Battle of Bosworth. Here in the grounds of Carew Castle Henry VII, who had been born in the nearby castle of Pembroke, celebrated the succession of a new dynasty by holding a great tournament in 1507. A mile away in a very different and altogether more peaceful setting is the church of Carew Cheriton (GR 046028).

The substantial church, with a very tall tower which must have been an important landmark in other days, stands in a very large churchyard, outside the gate of which survives a mounting block, while in the churchyard itself is to be found a very good assortment of old and interesting gravestones. Between the churchyard gate and the church is an unusual stone building, which has assumed two different and distinctive roles in the history of the parish. In many churchyards in the Middle Ages, when burial space became limited, it was customary to transfer the contents of older graves to a purpose-built charnel house, erected in the churchyard, where the bones were arranged in rows until the following All Hallow E'en when they were taken out and consumed in a parish bonfire, which in the beginning was known as a bone fire! Few of these charnel houses remain but the one at Carew Cheriton is in an excellent state of preservation because of the second role it was called upon to play in the eighteenth century, when it became the village school. It is interesting to speculate that the popularity accorded to bonfires after Guy Fawkes' unsuccessful attempt to blow up Parliament in 1605 may have been greatly increased by the earlier tradition of late autumnal bone fires, encouraged partly to get rid of the bones in overcrowded churchyards and partly to drive off the evil spirits which were believed to congregate at this time of year.

Eight miles north of Carew Cheriton the road joins the A40 at Conaston Bridge; two miles further north is Llawhaden (*Llanhuadain*, GR 076175), where in the sixth century the Christian missionary, Aidan, once the pupil of St David, found it possible to ford the river Cleddau and proceeded to enclose some land on which he built Llawhaden's first church. Centuries later, towards the end of the thirteenth century, on high ground well above the church by the river, the Bishop of St Davids saw fit to have a large house built which he then had fortified; this was indeed a bishop's castle, suited to the great status and affluence of a lord bishop. Even today its remains are most impressive. Gradually a village grew up near the castle, above the church, which is today linked to the village and the castle by an attractive stone bridge. The neighbourhood of the church in the Cleddau valley is pleasant indeed, far away from all clamour, as it must also have been in the Middle Ages, as the bishops had their own chapel in the castle. The large church, built in the thirteenth century, with many later additions, is sited very close to the river, near which a narrow path runs just behind the east wall of the church. Into the outside of this east wall has been built a Christian memorial stone, bearing a Latin cross, much eroded by the elements, thought to date from the tenth century. A short stay hereabouts, in castle and in churchyard, on a summer day will refresh the spirit as well as convey something of the social pattern of life in medieval times.

North west of Llawhaden through an intricate maze of minor roads or by main road seven miles north of Haverfordwest is the little church and churchyard of St Dogwells (*Llantydewi*, GR 969280). The church is dedicated to St Dogmael, whose patronal day was All Hallow E'en; very little else is known about him save that as there are several churches dedicated to him in old Pembrokeshire, he was probably a local Christian missionary. Access to the church, which is most agreeably situated in a well-wooded valley near a little stream is provided by an avenue of trees, yews and rhododendrons. In the churchyard there is evidence of the earlier Christian church here in the sixth century memorial stone, whose Latin and Ogham inscriptions are still visible despite the encroachment of vegetation.

Two miles inland from Abercastle on the west coast and eight miles north-east of St Davids and slightly to the west of the A487 is Mathri (GR 879320), which is an ideal place for historically-minded parents to take their children if ^{t'} ne is thought ripe for their historical education to begin! Mathri has been much lived in from prehistoric times to the present; a glance at the Ordnance Survey map will show that all roads lead to Mathri, while a walk round the churchyard, which is on top of the hill, will suggest that the church occupies a site that was probably used by Celts in the Iron Age for a hill-top settlement and used again later by the early Christian missionaries, who established a llan here, and yet again by men and women in the Middle Ages. The church is dedicated to the Seven Saints, who, according to local lore, were the seven sons born to a Pembrokeshire woman on the same day. Her impecunious husband, so the story goes, being quite unable to feed the unexpected number of mouths, took them to the river in order to drown them, when he was stopped in his tracks by none other than St Teilo, who persuaded him to hand them over. Thereafter they were reared and educated by Teilo and in adulthood came to Mathri to live — and to die, for, it is said, that as late as in 1720 their stone coffins were still being pointed out in the churchyard!

The present church was almost completely rebuilt in the nineteenth century but evidence of earlier Christian worship on the site survives in the raised, round nature of the churchyard and in the sixth century Christian memorial stone with Latin and Ogham inscriptions to be seen in the porch (formerly in the churchyard). In addition two seventh to ninth century memorial stones, bearing carved ringed crosses, which were found in local farms, have been built into the churchyard wall west of the church.

Llawhaden

Mathri — churchyard now a conservation area for wild flowers

B. Between Preseli and the Sea

The Strumble headland (Pen-caer), lying west of Fishguard, despite its rugged nature and its exposure to all the winds that blow, is dotted with evidence of prehistoric man's habitations; the easiest approach to it today in a car is up a twisting narrow road that runs steeply up behind Goodwick. On the top is the tiny village of Llanwnda (GR 932396); to this bleak area, where today, just inland from the wild west coast, there are a few scattered farms, Christian missionaries came and set up a llan, choosing this site presumably because there was a well nearby that had also enabled their prehistoric predecessors to make a settlement.

Of this first Christian church nothing survives except some gravestones and the llan itself. Today's simple Celtic church is old enough to have been in the care of Giraldus Cambrensis for a short while in the twelfth century. It was very carefully and successfully restored by the Victorians in 1870, when five memorial stones, which had been found in the llan, the present churchyard, were mortared into the outside walls of the church. These stones had marked early Christian burials somewhere between the seventh and ninth centuries.

By a strange quirk of chance this remote and unremarkable district had the spotlight of history turned upon it for a few days in February 1797, when a motley French invading force, of more than a thousand men, led by an American colonel, managed to get ashore and to climb the cliffs here and spread panic. This attempt at invasion became a farce as the undisciplined mob of soldiers roamed around, some of whom stole the communion plate from Llanwnda church, where two terrified girls cowered undetected in their hiding places. (The communion plate was later recovered and restored to the church.) Jemima Nicholas, the heroine of the moment, rounded up, with a pitchfork, in a field at Llanwnda some dozen French soldiers, a feat that is suitably remembered on her tombstone in the church at Fishguard. In London the threat implicit in this invasion attempt near Llanwnda was treated seriously enough for the Bank of England to suspend Cash Payments for the first time in its history.

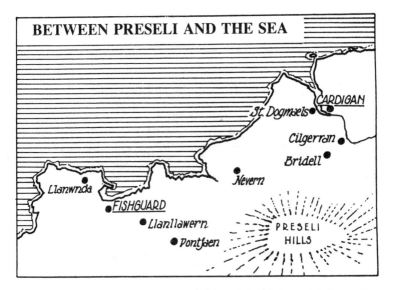

BETWEEN PRESELI AND THE SEA

CARDIGAN
St. Dogmaels
Cilgerran
Bridell
Nevern
Llanwnda
FISHGUARD
Llanllawern
Pontfaen
PRESELI
HILLS

Though little more than two miles inland from Fishguard, Llanllawern church (GR 987359) is remote and isolated and rather forlorn in appearance; it is unnamed even on the Ordnance Survey map. It can be found up a minor road off the B4313. Life seems to have stopped at Llanllawern but proofs are still at hand of human activitiy here in other days. The posts that support the entrance gate to the churchyard are twelve hundred years old, having originally marked the graves of early Christians who were buried in the llan. These stones, both unnamed, have carved upon them Latin crosses. Further evidence of early Christian and possibly of prehistoric settlement is provided by a well in the bottom of the neighbouring field, over which the coving has recently been restored. Marked as a Holy Well on the map, it had in former times a double reputation, for curing the sick and for carrying out curses, which were thought to follow the throwing of a bent pin into the water.

To reach Pontfaen (GR 022341) continue on the B4313 in a south-easterly direction away from Fishguard until GR 015334 is reached; here turn left on to a minor road for a further half mile. The church is dedicated to St Brynach, who probably set up the first llan in the sixth century when he was in charge at Nevern.

Though the little Celtic church was mostly rebuilt in Victorian times, the churchyard still contains along with many modern gravestones two memorial stones from very early times, both assigned to the seventh to the ninth centuries.

The churchyard at Nevern (*Nanhyfer*, GR 083401) is a veritable treasure haven for social historians, to some of whom it is the most exciting churchyard in the whole of Wales. The area around Nevern is so well favoured by nature with woods and wells and well-stocked streams that early man settled there from Neolithic times, Pentre Ifan, one of the best-known Neolithic sites in Britain, being only a mile or two from Nevern. The Irish Christian missionary St Brynach came to this hidden valley under its sheltering hill early in the sixth century and here enclosed a llan and built Nevern's first Christian place of worship. Whether Christian worship continued here without interruption it is not possible to say but there is every likelihood that the simple religious settlement became a clas with considerable influence in the valley.

Later, the Normans came here by sea to establish a base, building a castle on the hill above the church, of which only grass-covered earthworks remains. Down below in the former llan they built a stone church, but the tide of power soon passed away from Nevern when the Normans transferred their base to Newport, two miles away on the coast. Of the Norman church at Nevern probably only the tower remains, the rest of today's church having been added in the fifteenth century. At some time since then two fifth to sixth century gravestones, which were presumably still visible in the churchyard, were incorporated into the fabric of the church, both today in use as window sills on the south side of the nave. One is inscribed, in Latin and in Ogham, to Maglocunus, while the other is unnamed but bears in relief a cross, consisting of unusually intertwined stone cords. In addition high up in the outside wall on the north side is what appears to be the remaining portion of another early memorial stone, with the letters TVMIM still decipherable. As a middle nineteenth century church record refers to this particular stone as being in the south wall, it has to be presumed that it was removed to its present position in the great restoration of 1864.

Nevern — mounting block outside churchyard

St Dogmaels — church porch, enclosed yew tree and abbey ruins

Between the churchyard gate and the south porch of the church is an avenue of enormous yew trees, four on each side, with the second on the right famous locally as the 'bleeding' yew (a thick red substance suppurating from the spot where a branch was once cut off). Another twenty-six yews mark the southern boundary of the churchyard. Slightly to the east of the church porch is a memorial stone of the fifth to sixth century, marking, in Latin and in Ogham, the grave of Vitalianus Emeretus; this telling reminder of the early Christian llan is dwarfed by its proximity to Nevern's chief claim to historical fame, its tenth century Celtic Cross, which is as remarkable for its superb state of preservation as it is for its great height and expert decoration. Alone of the great Welsh crosses of this period Nevern's cross stands in the churchyard; it is not perhaps surprising that it figures prominently in local folk lore, often being connected with the patron saint, St Brynach, whose floruit, it is unsporting to remind readers, was four hundred years earlier!

To redress the balance attention has to be drawn to more modern features of the churchyard, such as eighteenth and nineteenth century gravestones, of which there are very many, more than a few of which are as outstanding for their shape and style as some of them are for their inscriptions. On the north east side of the churchyard there are two semi-enclosed burial grounds, partially walled-in, in one of which on its rear wall is an early nineteenth century memorial stone in remembrance of two infant children of the vicar. The striking epitaph runs thus:

> "They tasted of life's bitter cup,
> Refused to drink the potion up,
> But turned their little heads aside,
> Disgusted with the taste and died."

There are two further points of interest to be noted, both of them outside the churchyard. Pembrokeshire has two surviving mounting blocks outside churchyard gates; one has already been seen at Carew Cheriton, the other is here at Nevern. Finally a short distance west of the churchyard up a steep metalled road will be seen on the left hand side a notice Pilgrims' Cross. Follow a steep path to the left until a stile is reached, next to which is an oak tree; on the other side of the oak is a stone wall on which a number of crosses have been carved. Beneath the crosses is a groove, supposed to have been made by bent knees. This place is believed to be a wayside shrine, made by pilgrims on the last leg of their mighty pilgrimage from Holywell in Clwyd to St Davids.

St Dogmaels (*Llandudoch*, GR 164459) is a large village two miles south-west of Cardigan. Visitors come to St Dogmaels, the guide books insist, to see the ruins of the twelfth century abbey, now in State care. While it is also true to say that in times past a populous village grew up here because of the abbey, it has also to be stressed that Christianity came to these parts five hundred years before the foundation of the abbey. For here in the sixth century a Celtic missionary built a simple church in his llan, and it was in this already consecrated ground that the monastery was subsequently built. The present church, which was built in the nineteenth century in the remaining part of the original piece of consecrated ground, possesses a very important memorial stone from the original llan, commemorating one Sagranus, son of Cunotamus. On this stone is a very clear inscription in Ogham as well as in the customary Latin words. When finally scholars turned their attention to the vexed problem of trying to decipher this script, it was this particularly well-preserved stone from St Dogmaels which enabled them to succeed to 1848.

Any churchyard which has had an abbey built in it must be thought worth a visit! These ruins of St Mary's Abbey certainly repay systematic study. Between the south door of the church and the north entrance to the abbey ruins should be noted a very old ycw, which is so large that it has had a three feet high brick wall built to contain it.

C. In old Cardiganshire

On a hill overlooking the sea between Cardigan and New Quay is Penbryn (GR 294522); the church is fittingly dedicated to St Michael, its original name having been Llanfihangel-ar-y-bryn. Whether there was an early Celtic missionary settlement here is not known, as no contemporary gravestone has been unearthed in the churchyard, though half a mile away in a field an early Christian memorial stone survives with its interesting inscription intact. Certainly the roundness of the churchyard suggests an early llan on the site but may have to be accounted for by the comment in the church notes that "the churchyard was made circular rather than square so that there would be no hiding place in the corners for the Devil!"In a churchyard which has many interesting gravestones, including large and distinctive eighteenth century specimens, pride of place must go to the grave of a nineteenth century vicar, who was buried under the yew tree at the bottom of the churchyard. In the Rebecca Riots some years before his death he had fallen foul of the rioters; as at his death some protection was still thought necessary, a very heavy stone cross was placed upon his grave, which was securely fenced off by strong iron railings.

In the Rheidol valley, a mile east of Aberystwyth (of which it is now virtually a part) stands the church of Llanbadarn Fawr (GR 599810). Here in the sixth century St David's contemporary, St Padarn set up the first Christian church in the district, a simple church which later became a clas, whose reputation as a centre of Christianity and learning spread far and wide. This early church was destroyed in a Viking raid but survivors of those early days of Christian monasticism are to be seen and admired in the south transept of today's church, which is richly embellished with two excellent examples of Celtic crosses. With today's church, which dates from the twelfth century, Wales' greatest medieval poet, Dafydd ap Gwilym has associations, though not of a particularly poetic nature. As a young man he came to worship in this church, but according to contemporary opinion his attention was centred more on the girls in the congregation than on the holy words of the presiding

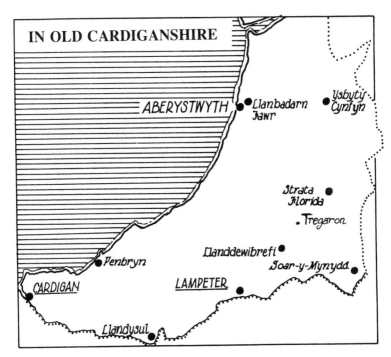

IN OLD CARDIGANSHIRE

ABERYSTWYTH • Llanbadarn Jawr   • Ysbyty Cynfyn

Strata Florida •

• Tregaron

Llanddewibrefi •

Soar-y-Mynydd •

Penbryn •

LAMPETER •

CARDIGAN

Llandysul •

priest! Earlier in this book reference was made to the poet's grave in the churchyard of the church next to Strata Florida Abbey, where the great yew planted on his grave has flourished exceedingly.

Much further south, between Lampeter and Newcastle Emlyn is Llandysul (GR 418407), seemingly a thriving community today thanks to the woollen industry, which is centred in half a dozen mills in the neighbouring countryside, all of which depend for water power on tributaries of the river Teifi, in whose valley Llandysul grew up. In quite a different way the river was responsible for there being a settlement here at all, because in the fifth century the Teifi could be forded here, encouraging the Celtic missionary Tysul to enclose a llan and to build a rudimentary church, which in later times was supplanted by a large stone building, similarly dedicated to St Tysul.

Inside the church today, in the north wall of the tower is an important pointer to the time when Llandysul had a thriving monastic community in its llan, part of a memorial stone which dates from the sixth century, along with part of a Latin inscription. This so called Velvor stone is all that remains of an inscribed slab, which presumably once marked a local grave. According to existing records, at one time this slab formed part of the stile that led into the churchyard, before it was moved to another position in the churchyard wall near the entrance gate.

As in many another Welsh churchyard ball games were popular here, especially the playing of fives against the tower of the church; in Llandysul churchyard however there was another popular athletic activity, trying to throw a ball over the tall church tower. It is believed that this considerable feat was only accomplished on one occasion, namely by a sexton in the early years of the eighteenth century. There was too yet another ball game popular hereabouts until about a hundred and fifty years ago, when a strong-minded vicar put a stop to it. On New Year's Day the men and boys of the parish used to participate in a ball game against their opposite numbers in the parish of Llanwenog, six miles away. This fast and furious game started at a halfway point and the two goals were the respective church porches of Llanwenog and Llandysul.

Llanddewibrefi (GR 664554) is situated under the lee of the Cambrian Mountains, on the B4343 between Tregaron and Lampeter; it deserves to be a special place of pilgrimage for all Welsh people who are possessed of a sense of their ancient heritage and indeed for all other Britons who can be moved by the evidence of the early days of Christianity in these islands. This historic village on the river Teifi is indeed hallowed ground for the historian; here there is a great awareness of the past, a past that extends back further than to the time of St David as the Romans passed that way, building themselves a military outpost on the other side of the river at Pontllanio; maybe Llanddewi's past goes back further still because St David's parish church was built on a round and raised mound on which there is every reason to think, but no available evidence to prove, that the people of the Bronze Age lived and died there many centuries before.

A different explanation for the raised nature of the site was once proffered by the earliest biographer of St David, Rhigfarch

Llanddewi Brefi — the raised churchyard

Llanbadarn Fawr — where Dafydd ap Gwilym eyed the girls

169

in the late eleventh century. The young David, present there in the churchyard at a synod of the church, in the sixth century, according to his biographer, when called upon for an opinion, replied with such eloquence and authority that the very ground on which he stood rose up, symbolising to all present his superiority over all the other members of the synod! This story is of particular interest, coming five hundred years after the alleged event; for, in the eleventh century the author's father, Sulien, who was Bishop of St Davids, was fighting hard to prevent his diocese from passing under the jurisdiction of the see of Canterbury.

Today's stone church, fittingly dedicated to St David, was built about 1200 on the top of the mound in the llan; nothing of any earlier building has survived though memorial stones from the churchyard were brought into the church in the nineteenth century, when a thorough rebuilding of the nave and chancel became necessary. Of the original church of 1200 only the stout tower survives. In 1696 Edward Lhuyd, the great Welsh scholar, who became the Keeper of the Ashmolean Museum at Oxford, visited Llanddewi in the course of an extensive tour of Wales, gathering relevant information for his monumental work, *Archaeologia Britannica*, which was published in 1707. At Llanddewi Lhuyd saw and marvelled at the Idnert Stone; posterity has every reason to be grateful to Lhuyd for writing down what he saw because today less than half the stone which he saw is available for us to see. In the rebuilding of the nave and chancel in the nineteenth century a stonemason trimmed and cut down this stone before using it to fill a gap in the outside wall of the nave. This early Christian stone recorded the murder of Idnert, the Abbot of the monastery of Llanbadarn Fawr; the inscription in addition contains the earliest known mention of St David himself. The surviving two pieces of this stone may still be seen from the churchyard high up in the outside wall of the nave, although one piece was inserted upside down. Inside the church under the tower are the memorial stones previously referred to as having been brought in from the churchyard; they relate to the time of the first simple building in the llan, one of the stones having an inscription in Ogham as well as in Latin. Interesting as are these reminders in the tower of early days, it is especially in the churchyard that the sense of the past is strongest. On the south side a very ancient yew, growing out of a low round mound speaks of other times, when the founder of the Christian church in Wales himself took part here in public debate.

A brief stop is recommended about four miles north of Llanddewi at the little market town of Tregaron (GR 680599), a favourite spot for those interested in the treasures to be found there in the largest peat bog in Britain. To this place in the sixth century there came an Irish Christian missionary, Caron, who, attracted by a mound immediately above the river Teifi, established a llan in which he built a wooden church. Today's church, which is mostly a nineteenth century building apart from its sturdy medieval tower, stands on the top of this impressive steep mound, whose considerable slopes have been entirely filled with burial stones. This early date, ascribed to Tregaron's first Christian church, found ample confirmation at the beginning of the nineteenth century, when four sixth century memorial stones were discovered; they were later displayed inside the church tower until they were taken away from Tregaron. Two of them, however, are today in the care of the National Museum in Cardiff.

This survey of churchyards ends in Ysbyty Cynfyn (GR 752791), which is twelve miles east of Aberystwyth and two miles north of Devil's Bridge, under the western slopes of Pumlumon (*Plynlimon*). When George Borrow visited the district in the middle of the nineteenth century he took the church to be a Methodist chapel because it was only about thirty years old. However, if the building belongs to the nineteenth century, the churchyard most certainly is ancient. In fact there is no churchyard in Wales where there is a longer history of burial or where there is so obvious an example of the continuity of the religious use of one particular site.

A llan was probably established here in the early years of the Christian missionary movement in Wales; by the twelfth century there was a stone church, which provided a hospice, as Ysbyty indicates, for travellers en route to the Cistercian monastery of Strata Florida, which is twelve miles to the south. This churchyard at Ysbyty Cynfyn was briefly mentioned earlier in this book when churchyards built on prehistoric sites were being considered. All the churches built in this place, from the earliest religious settlement in the llan to the present early nineteenth century edifice, have stood inside a Bronze Age alignment of stones. This calculated choice of sites by early Christians adds weight to the arguments of those who believe that in former times great importance was attached to the magic powers associated with circles. Some have argued that the very roundness of a churchyard gave to many people a sense of security, a feeling that no harm could come to the dead, who were buried within the protection of the circle. Readers who may be interested in this idea might care to ponder further upon the origin of round games and bear in mind the stress laid even up to a century or so ago on the ritual of "clipping" the church, when parishoners, sometimes adults, sometimes children, gathered in the churchyard and joined hands before gradually moving nearer to the church, where the priest awaited them at the entrance to the building. Be that as it may, the present-day churchyard wall at Ysbyty Cynfyn contains five stones that belonged to a Bronze Age circle, of which probably three are still in their original positions, the other two having at some time been moved to act as gate posts. There are no ifs and buts about Ysbyty Cynfyn, which provides an impressive example of the continuity of religious association in a burial ground.

Tregaron — church on top of a mound

Ysbyty Cynfyn — bronze age stone in churchyard wall

173

BIBLIOGRAPHY

Of the many works of reference consulted, the following four books stand out as indispensable.

Bowen, E.G., *The Settlements of the Celtic Saints of Wales*.
Giraldus Cambrensis, *Itinerary of Wales*.
Jones, Francis, *The Holy Wells of Wales*.
Nash-Williams, V.E., *The Early Christian Monuments of Wales*.

ACKNOWLEDGEMENTS

The following are the owners of the copyright of the illustrations and have kindly permitted their use.

Royal Commission on Ancient and Historical Monuments in Wales *(Crown Copyright)*
On pages 47a and 75b.

Cambridge University
On pages 25b and 79

Peter Haviland, Falcon Studios, Penmachno
On page 37a

Emrys Jones
On page 77

Gwasg Carreg Gwalch
On pages 5a, 11a and b, 19b, 29a, 33, 75a, 83a and b, 85a and b.

The rest of the photographs were taken by my wife and are her copyright.

INDEX OF PLACE NAMES

Aberdaron...................... 71, 77, 78
Aberedw.............. 113, 115, 116, 119
Aberhafhesb 95
Barclodiad-y-gawres 10
Bardsey (*Ynys Enlli*) 71, 72, 78, 79
Beguildy 103, 104, 107
Berriew (*Aberriw*) 72, 95, 100, 101
Betws-y-coed 81, 85
Bishopston 145, 146
Bleddfa........................... 103, 109
Bosherton 48, 153
Bridell 37, 38, 161
Bryn Celli Ddu................ 10, 11, 63
Caergybi 25, 26
Caerhun......................... 24, 25, 81
Caer-went 24, 129
Capel Garmon 10, 11
Carew Cheriton 153, 155, 156
Casgob 103, 109, 110
Castell Collen 23
Cefnllys 112, 113
Cerrig Ceinwen..................... 28, 63
Cheriton 149, 150
Cilcain 89
Cilgerran...................... 36, 37, 161
Clocaenog 53, 89
Clynnog Fawr 49, 71, 72, 73, 75
Coety 139, 143, 144
Corwen................. 22, 80, 81, 82, 83
Coychurch 48, 139, 143
Cwmdu 37, 48, 121, 124, 125
Cwmyoy.................... 121, 129, 130
Cymer Abbey 86
Derwen.............................. 48, 89
Diserth (*Disserth*)... 113, 114, 115, 117
Ewenny Priory.......................... 49
Fishguard 161
Four Stones............................ 20
Ffynnon Non 33, 34
Glasgwm............... 7, 18, 56, 58, 113
Gresford 42, 89
Grosmont.. 48, 129, 130, 131, 132, 133
Guilsfield (*Cegidfa*) 95, 97, 99
Gwytherin 19, 22, 35, 81
Halkyn 30, 89
Hanmer 47, 48, 89
Heyhop........................... 103, 104
Holywell 27, 89
Ilston............................. 145, 152

Kerry (*Ceri*) 95, 102
Knighton........................... 31, 105
Llanaelhaearn 35, 71, 73, 74
Llananno...................... 103, 106
Llanarmon Dyffryn Ceiriog...... 89, 92
Llanarmon-yn-Iâl............. 89, 90, 91
Llanbadarn Fawr
(Dyfed)............... 166, 167, 169, 170
Llanbadarn Fawr
(Powys) 23, 113, 122
Llanbadarn Fynydd....... 103, 105, 106
Llanbadarn-y-Garreg 113, 118
Llanbadrig........................... 63, 68
Llanbedr Ystrad Yw...... 121, 124, 126
Llanbeblig 24
Llanbister............. 103, 106, 107, 108
Llancarfan 139, 142
Llanddeiniolen 42, 81
Llanddew, Powys 121, 122
Llanddewibrefi 167, 168, 169
Llanddewi, Gower... 49, 145, 147, 152
Llanddwywe 7, 8
Llandeloy 33, 153
Llandyfalle 53, 121, 126
Llandrindod Wells ... 31, 103, 112, 113
Llandwrog.............................. 21
Llandysul 167, 168
Llaneilian 48, 63, 67, 69
Llanelltud............................ 81, 86
Llanerfyl 39, 95
Llanfaes 63, 65, 68, 70
Llanfair-ar-y-Bryn 23
Llanfair Caereinion............... 31, 95
Llanfair Isgoed
(*Llanfair Discoed*) 53, 124
Llanfair Dyffryn Clwyd 89, 91, 93
Llanfechain.................... 95, 96, 99
Llanfigan (*Llanfeugan*) .. 121, 123, 125
Llanfihangel-ar-Arth.................. 39
Llanfihangel Nant Melan.... 18, 42, 43
Llanfihangel Rhydieithon..... 103, 109
Llanfilo.................................. 48
Llangadwaladr........ 38, 39, 63, 64, 69
Llangaffo 63, 64
Llangan 46, 139, 141, 143, 144
Llangedwyn 36
Llangelynnin 28, 29, 30, 81, 82, 83
Llangennith 29, 145, 147,
148, 149, 150

Llangernyw.......................... 35, 81
Llangïan.............................. 35, 71
Llangwm, Clwyd 5
Llangwm, Dyfed 5
Llangwm, Gwent............. 5, 129, 136
Llangwnnadl 71, 77, 78
Llanhamlach 86, 123
Llanidan 63, 66
Llanilltud Fawr
(*Llantwit Major*) 138, 139, 140, 141
Llanllawern 38, 161
Llanmadoc 145, 150
Llanrhidian................ 145, 150, 151
Llanrhychwyn 81, 84, 85
Llansadwrn.......................... 39, 63
Llansantffraid-yn-Elfael............. 42
Llansbyddid 36
Llansilin.......................... 89, 90, 93
Llanwnda 160, 161
Llanwrthwl 20, 113
Llanynys 88, 89
Llawhaden............ 153, 156, 157, 159
Maentwrog 19, 21, 81
Maes-yr-onnen 57, 58, 59, 121
Manorbier 153, 154, 155
Mathri 153, 157, 158, 159
Meidrim.................................. 17
Meifod.......................... 95, 98, 100
Montgomery 42, 95, 96
Nanhoron........................... 60, 71
Nantmel........................... 113, 114
Nevern .. 36, 46, 47, 161, 162, 163, 164
Old Radnor.................... 18, 20, 103

Overton 44, 89
Oxwich 32, 86, 145
Pales, Llandegley 56, 57, 103
Partrishow.............. 47, 48, 121, 124,
                          126, 127, 128
Penally 153, 154
Penbryn 166, 167
Pencelli 123
Penmachno................. 35, 37, 38, 81
Penmon 63
Penrhos Llugwy 62, 63
Pentre Ifan............................. 10
Pilleth.............................. 31, 103
Pistyll 71, 75, 76
Pontfaen 38, 161
Rhosili........................ 49, 145, 147
Rhulen 113, 117, 118, 119, 120
St Dogmaels
(*Llandudoch*) 161, 163, 165
St Dogwells.................. 38, 153, 157
St Donats 48, 139, 140, 141
St Mary Hill 48, 139, 143, 144
Skenfrith 129, 132, 133, 134
Soar-y-Mynydd.......... 59, 60, 61, 167
Strata Florida 43, 44, 167
Tenby.................................. 153
Tinkinswood 10
Treflys.................................. 38
Tregaron.................... 167, 171, 173
Tregynon 49, 95, 96
Trelawnyd (*Newmarket*) 48
Trelech (Tryleg). 47, 129, 134, 135, 137
Ysbyty Cynfyn 167, 171, 172, 173

COUNTRY CHURCHYARDS
IN WALES